THE MIND IS A LABYRINTH WITH THREE KEYS

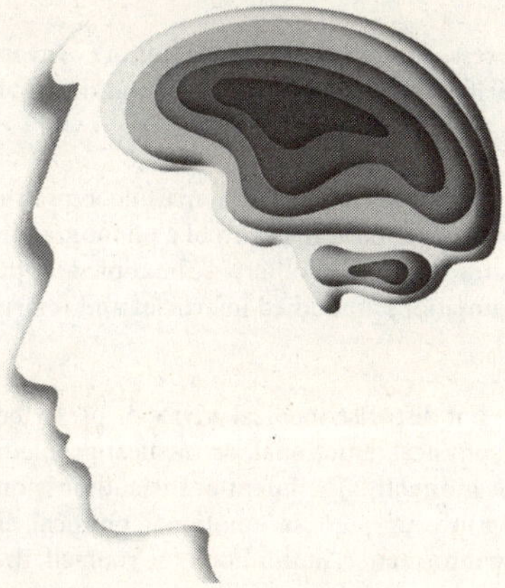

Unlock the Secrets *of the* Conscious, Unconscious *and* Superconscious

GURDIP HARI

HAY HOUSE

HAY HOUSE INDIA
New Delhi • London • Sydney
Carlsbad, California • New York City

Hay House Publishers (India) Pvt Ltd
Muskaan Complex, Plot No. 3, B-2, Vasant Kunj, New Delhi – 110070, India

Hay House LLC, P.O. Box 5100, Carlsbad, CA 92018-5100, USA
Hay House UK Ltd, 1st Floor, Crawford Corner, 91-93 Baker Street, London W1U 6QQ, UK
Hay House Australia Publishing Pty Ltd, 18/36 Ralph St., Alexandria NSW 2015, Australia

Email: contact@hayhouse.co.in
Website: www.hayhouse.co.in

First published by Hay House India, 2025
Reprint, 2026
11 10 9 8 7 6 5 4 3 2

ISBN 978-93-6611-797-3 (Paperback)
ISBN 978-93-6611-603-7 (Ebook)

Printed at Thomson Press India Private Limited

FSC
www.fsc.org
MIX
Paper | Supporting responsible forestry
FSC® C010615

Hay House is committed to a sustainable future for our business, our readers and our planet. This book is made from Forest Stewardship Council® certified paper.

A Sacred Offering

This special edition of 1100 copies is offered in devotion to the Parents, Teachers, and Pupils of *Guru Harkrishan Public Schools, Delhi*. It stands as a living companion on your shared pilgrimage of learning and as one sacred side of the eternal coin of *Oneness*.

Why 1100 copies? Guru Nanak Sahib revealed the luminous truth of *Ik Onkar*, that the Creator is One. We are born as reflections of that One, yet our journey unfolds through mind and heart, one and one, until through awareness and love they reunite into the original *Oneness*. The 11 reflects this sacred union, while the 00 whispers of infinity, with no beginning and no end.

Within these pages lives a divine map for becoming a true *Sikh of Oneness*, a lifelong seeker who never ceases to learn and remains forever open to growth, wonder, and awakening. The living wisdom of *Man jeetai jag jeet* unfolds gently, guiding the reader to victory over the mind and into the discovery of the vast inner universe within.

When woven into the fabric of a school's curriculum, this book becomes a vessel of *Inner Science* and a bridge of language enhancement. Through it, thought learns to sing and words become instruments of light. Both the written and spoken English language rise into mastery, helping young souls grow into confident global citizens who can offer their talents, their voices, and their wisdom of *Oneness* to the world.

May this book walk beside every parent, teacher, and pupil as a silent teacher, awakening self-awareness, nurturing purpose, and guiding each learner toward their highest divine potential, until every mind and every heart finds its way to the *Oneness* of *Ik Onkar*.

This work is dedicated to my beloved father, who departed for the realm we call heaven in March of the year two thousand, and became my guiding light. Every endeavour I have undertaken since the day he physically left this earthly realm has been guided by his presence in spirit. That, to me, is love—or rather true eternal love—ever-present, all-encompassing, and permeating every fibre of my being. I offer this work as a tribute to that love, which resides within you, within me, and within all of creation, for we are undeniably interconnected, part of that divine unity we call God or nature, the wellspring from which our existence emanates.

Contents

Preface

In the intricate weave of ancient scriptures, three states of consciousness are interwoven with myriad threads of timeless wisdom. The sacred texts of India define these core aspects of human nature as *sattvic, rajasic,* and *tamasic.* Similarly, the Bible, the Quran, and other holy texts echo these states, describing them as virtuous, ambitious, and ignorant. Each state reflects varying levels of awareness corresponding to different facets of an individual's mind and profoundly influences behaviour, thought processes, and the fabric of life experiences. Delving into these states unveils mystical insights into human psychology and the path to holistic growth on earth—the singular school of learning to which we return repeatedly, evolving through each lifetime until we achieve spiritual graduation.

The sattvic or virtuous state harmonises with the superconscious mind, epitomising the pinnacle of awareness and enlightenment. This state is a sanctuary of wisdom, inner peace, and a profound connection with the inner self. Here, the mind transcends the ego and material desires, focusing instead on self-realisation and the holistic growth of mind, body, and spirit. Individuals dwelling in this state, depending on their level of awareness, embody selflessness, compassion, and a sense of duty. Their actions are infused with the intent to benefit others, motivated by love, truth, and justice. Guided by discernment and a deep understanding of the interconnectedness of all life, they lead disciplined and ethical lives. Their paths are marked by the pursuit of knowledge and selfless giving, as they become beacons of light in the world.

The rajasic or ambitious state is intimately connected with the conscious mind, where the fires of desire, ambition, and the pursuit of achievement burn brightly. This state is characterised by dynamism and ceaseless activity, often birthing stress and dissatisfaction when the vast spectrum of never-ending desires remains unfulfilled. Individuals in this state, depending on their level of awareness, are propelled by personal goals and motivations. They are energetic, ambitious, and competitive, seeking power, fame, and material success. Yet, this relentless pursuit can lead to overwork, anxiety, and an insatiable yearning. Their actions, driven by ego and the pursuit of pleasure, often ensnare them in cycles of attachment and suffering, creating a tempest within their souls.

The tamasic or ignorant state corresponds with the unconscious mind, shrouded in confusion, ignorance, and resistance to change. This state is a realm of stagnation and delusion, where progress is a distant echo. In this state, the mind is clouded, making it difficult to see beyond immediate, often self-destructive gratifications. Ancient texts lament that people perish due to a lack of knowledge, highlighting the peril of remaining in this state. Individuals enmeshed in this state, depending on their level of awareness, exhibit laziness, apathy, procrastination, and a tendency for destructive behaviours. They are often driven by fear, superstition, and a fog of misunderstanding. This state can spiral into depression, addiction, and a pervasive sense of hopelessness. Their actions, harmful to both themselves and others, stem from a disconnection from the higher purpose of life and a lack of clarity in their minds. And in order to move beyond this state of ignorance and despair, one must awaken to the higher laws that govern existence—the timeless principles that remind us that our actions, like seeds, inevitably bear fruit.

Our earthly sojourn is governed by the mystical and timeless law of sow and reap, which encapsulates the essence of planting seeds and reaping a bountiful harvest. In essence, our actions are the seeds we plant, and the resulting outcomes signify the harvest we reap. Every divine scripture elucidates the sacred law of giving, intrinsically linked to sowing, even the earth herself demands our seeds to bestow upon us her corresponding fruits. The reality of our existence is enshrined in the act of giving, a cosmic principle mirrored in the formation of the human body. The union of a sperm and an egg serves as a sublime metaphor for this, where male and female partners each offer a part of themselves to create new life. This union is an act of divine selflessness and cosmic collaboration, symbolising the ultimate gift of creation.

Once conception occurs, the mother's body becomes an automatic vessel of continuous giving. For nine months, nourishment, protection, and an environment for the fetus to grow unfold effortlessly. This period of gestation is marked by a profound exchange of energy and resources, embodying the principle of giving in its purest form. The act of birth is another profound expression of giving, where the mother endures the pains of labour to bring forth new life. The newborn, in turn, emerges as a gift to the world, embodying potential and hope through the continuity of the human race and the soul's eternal journey.

This reinforces the ageless truth that we are here to give and serve one another—a divine principle beautifully illustrated through the act of pregnancy. Once a child is conceived, the subsequent stages of birth unfold as a natural, pre-programmed process governed by the inherent wisdom of creation. However, the future development and character of that child are significantly influenced by the state of consciousness of the two individuals who contributed to the seed, as well as the upbringing and nurturing they will provide. The law of giving stipulates that the quality of our gifts will correspond to the state of consciousness we inhabit.

In the celestial dance of life, the virtuous, or superconscious state, aligns with the highest vibrations of giving. Here, individuals sow seeds of purity, love, and selfless service, yielding a harvest of peace, eternal success, and divine fulfillment. In this state, the heart and mind are in perfect harmony with the cosmic rhythms, and actions are driven by an unwavering sense of duty, compassion, and truth. The gifts born from this state are luminous, uplifting the soul and resonating with the light of higher wisdom. Virtuous individuals move through life as vessels of divine grace, their actions a testament to the interconnectedness of all beings.

In contrast, the ambitious, or conscious state, aligns with desire and the relentless pursuit of achievement. Here, the seeds sown are those of effort, ambition, and often ego-driven intentions. The harvest is one of material success, recognition, and personal gratification, but it is also accompanied by stress, dissatisfaction, and the ceaseless yearning for more. In this state, giving is often transactional, motivated by the expectation of returns or the enhancement of one's status. The gifts arising from the ambitious state are dynamic and impactful, yet they may lack the purity and depth of those emanating from the virtuous realm. The ambitious individual is a force of change and progress, but their journey is marked by the dualities of gain and loss, pleasure and pain.

The ignorant (unconscious state) aligns with the lowest vibrations of giving. Here, the seeds are those of neglect, apathy, and destructive tendencies. The harvest is a barren field of stagnation, despair, and suffering. In this state, giving is of an unconscious nature, as the individual is often consumed by fear, superstition, and a lack of understanding. The gifts that emerge from this state are tainted by negativity and ignorance, causing harm to both the giver and the receiver. Ignorant individuals are entangled in a web of illusions, their actions mired in confusion and delusion, leading to a life of missed opportunities and unfulfilled potential.

The mystical journey of giving across these three states reveals the transformative power of our intentions and actions. When we give from a place of unconsciousness, our gifts may hinder rather than help, often perpetuating dependency or harm. When we give consciously, we empower and uplift the lives of many, fostering growth and self-sufficiency. But when we give from a superconscious state, we transcend the limitations of the material world, offering the gift of eternal wisdom through divine leadership, leading to an abundance of the highest order.

Moreover, the divine interplay of these three states of consciousness shapes not only the lives of parents and children but also the very fabric of our existence and the nature of our contributions to the world. By understanding and aligning ourselves with the higher realms of being, we can transform our lives, the lives of future generations, and those around us.

Put simply, the law of sow and reap is not merely a cosmic mandate but a sacred pathway to self-realisation, supernatural success, and ultimate harmony in every sphere of life. This eternal principle has not only been echoed in sacred scriptures but also found voice in art and music, reminding humanity of its timeless relevance.

In the final musical contribution of the famed Beatles, the album titled *Abbey Road,* we encounter a line of prophetic wisdom: 'And in the end, the love you take is equal to the love you make.' These words, sung with a sense of closing finality, encapsulate a profound and divine essence that resonates deeply with universal truths about eternal existence, consciousness, and the nature of love.

At the heart of this lyric is the timeless principle of reciprocity, which echoes ancient spiritual and philosophical teachings across cultures and epochs. This principle, akin to the law of sow and reap, suggests that the energy we emit into the universe—in the form of thoughts, actions, and, most crucially, love—inevitably returns to us in equal measure. This is not merely a poetic notion but a reflection of the timeless law of balance and continuity that governs the cosmos. Across various spiritual traditions, this concept is central, emphasising that our deeds, whether positive or negative, create a ripple effect that ultimately shapes our destiny. For instance, Rumi, the 13th-century Persian poet and Sufi mystic, often spoke of love as the essence of eternal life, and wrote, 'Love is the bridge between you and everything.'

When a soul finally departs from the physical body, the actions or seeds sown throughout its lifetime become instrumental in constructing the bridge to its next existence. This bridge, forged from the essence of one's deeds, thoughts, talents, and intentions, determines the soul's journey and the circumstances of its future incarnations. And in each new incarnation, life unfurls intricately through hereditary elements, seamlessly weaving the soul's past into the fabric of its present life. The soul is drawn to a family and environment—often involving children and grandchildren—where hereditary traits and conditions align with its previous patterns, ensuring that the lessons and experiences necessary for its continued evolution and learning are present.

This process reflects the profound and mystical law of cosmic justice, where every action bears fruit and every soul reaps the harvest of its past deeds. The soul's journey is a continuum, with each life serving as a chapter in an eternal story of growth, learning, and self-realisation. The familial and genetic circumstances into which a soul is born are not mere coincidences but deliberate alignments orchestrated by the divine law.

In this context, heredity serves as the channel through which destiny manifests. The soul, carrying the imprints of its past actions, thoughts, and talents, gravitates towards a lineage that allows these imprints to find expression. This ensures that the soul encounters situations and relationships that mirror its inner state, providing opportunities for advancement on its path of learning.

A compelling illustration of this principle is seen in the life of Avirbhav, a seven-year-old prodigy who emerged victorious in the Superstar Singer Contest in August 2024, a prestigious musical event hosted by Sony Entertainment Television, India. This contest is designed to discover and nurture young talent across the nation, offering participants rigorous training to hone their vocal abilities and preparing them for the international stage.

Avirbhav's extraordinary musical prowess was no mere coincidence but a manifestation of his eternal journey. Born into a family steeped in musical tradition—his father a classical musician, and his mother a vocalist—Avirbhav was naturally drawn into an environment where his latent talents could flourish. This familial background, perfectly aligned with imprints from his previous lifetimes, provided the ideal foundation for him to refine and elevate his inherent musical abilities. His triumph in the national contest, where he outshone contestants significantly older than himself, speaks volumes about his extraordinary skills at such a tender age. His performances were marked by a soulful voice that carried a depth of emotion and an impressive versatility across various musical genres. These qualities resonated deeply with audiences worldwide, creating a powerful emotional connection that transcended age and experience.

Avirbhav's story is not just about a young boy winning a contest; it is a profound testament to the convergence of past life experiences, familial support, and the unfolding of destiny in shaping one's life. His victory underscores the idea that the talents and abilities we possess are not limited to a single lifetime but are the fruits of efforts and experiences accumulated over many lifetimes. It is a reminder that each soul's journey is unique, intricately woven with the threads of destiny, heredity, and the environment into which we are born, ultimately guiding us towards our chosen paths.

This interplay of birth and heredity also highlights the interconnectedness of all life, underscoring the soul's perpetual journey towards higher consciousness and realisation of its inherent talents and divine powers. Each incarnation is a step forward on this sacred path, where the soul, through its experiences and actions, gradually purifies itself and aligns more closely with the universal principles of love, compassion, and wisdom. Thus, the cycle of birth, death, and rebirth is not a random occurrence but a purposeful process. As the soul evolves, it traverses various lifetimes, each meticulously crafted to further its evolutionary growth. Familial ties and inherited tendencies serve as tools through which the universe facilitates this journey, aligning each incarnation with opportunities for growth and ultimate graduation from the earthly realm. In essence, understanding the intricate reality of our eternal existence and the universal law of sow and reap forms the foundation for deeper self-awareness and authentic learning. By recognising how past actions and hereditary influences shape our present, we can perceive the vast tapestry of the soul's journey.

Moving forward, this book will illuminate the soul's journey from birth in each incarnation. It will delve into why we are the way we are and offer insights into transforming thought patterns and habitual conditioning. Through an in-depth exploration of the mind's three transformative states—the conscious, unconscious, and superconscious—you will gain a clearer understanding of your psychological blueprint. This awareness aids in aligning habits with divine laws, deepening your grasp of how these ingrained actions impact life's roles, from childhood to parenthood and into grandparenthood. Recognising and transforming these behaviours is essential for breaking free from cycles of repetitive patterns that lead to suffering, poor health, misfortune, and financial instability. Here, it is worth noting that the sacred law of life operates in duality: change your habits to elevate your consciousness and empower yourself, or remain bound within cycles of mediocrity.

The book will also guide you on how to harmonise thoughts, words, and actions, rooted in the divine wisdom that creation itself began with a thought. This is crucial as thoughts evolve into words, words lead to actions, actions solidify as habits, and habits ultimately shape character. Understanding this sequence is essential, for it reveals how the invisible realm of thought gradually manifests into the tangible reality of our lives.

We should also keep in mind that at every moment, the eternal power of contemplation, the voice of expression, and the profound sense of ownership reside within us. In parallel with God's grant of free will, these principles enable us to consciously choose and manifest our desires, guided by the law of sow and reap, which allows us to shape our destiny in alignment with our sovereign will.

Building on this truth, the pages ahead invite you to apply these principles in your own life, setting the stage for self-discovery and transformation. By comprehending the workings of your mind and aligning your thoughts and actions with divine laws, you can liberate yourself from the chains of ingrained patterns. The practical tools provided in this book will empower you to heal, grow, and transform every aspect of your life.

Overall, in embracing this journey, you are not only seeking personal enlightenment but also contributing to the continued upliftment of the collective evolution of humanity. Each step you take towards your own metamorphosis ripples out into the world, inspiring others to follow their path to mental, physical, spiritual, and financial fulfillment. This sacred journey is an invitation to transcend the ordinary and step into a life of extraordinary grace and purpose.

The Silent Whisper of Dawn

This work is a timeless gift from eternity,
For parents, teachers, and pupils,
To embark on a journey
Of lifelong learning and infinite discovery.

And so, the eternal truth stands tall,
Humbly proclaiming,
That each of us, in every moment,
Is a pupil, a teacher, a parent—
A lifelong learner,
Walking the sacred path of wisdom.

Through seeking, learning, and evolving,
We unveil the divinity within,
Until we rise beyond illusion,
Merging into the oneness
That has always been.

Introduction

In the vast tapestry of human existence, a captivating enigma has persistently perplexed the psyches of historians, philosophers, and psychologists throughout the ages. This enigma, unrivaled in its singular essence and known as the human mind, unveils itself as a labyrinth of intricate nerves, whose inner workings and profound complexity have unnerved the entirety of humankind. And within this labyrinth of the human mind, as we look across a world teeming with billions of souls, dwelling within diverse nations, cultures, and circumstances, the most significant reality of our being resonates: No two minds are forged alike. While it is comprehensible that divergences arise from dissimilarities in culture, language, and geographical milieu, a mystery remains shrouded in the confines of a family unit. How is it that within the intimate embrace of a single roof, the minds of a kin remain resolutely distinctive? This baffling facet of the human mind tantalises our collective curiosity, evading comprehension throughout the annals of our shared history.

Here, it is important to recognise that the conventional factors of nation, culture, or language, in fact, hold no dominion. The essence of individuality manifests in radiant splendour, unbounded by external trappings. It is a testament to the awe-inspiring diversity that permeates our very essence, whispering the vast kaleidoscope of human consciousness. Thus, the great riddle endures, enticing us to unravel its enigmatic threads and beckoning us to explore the boundless depths of the human psyche.

Yet, amidst this captivating quest, we encounter the greatest of challenges—our minds incessantly resist dwelling in the present moment. Instead, they relentlessly pull us, as if caught in a turbulent tide, either towards the haunting clutches of the past or the tantalising allure of the future.

So, to better grasp the inner workings of the mind, let us draw a parallel to the workings of a computer. While a computer necessitates the deliberate input of information, the mind ceaselessly gathers data automatically, without any conscious effort or time investment. From the tender years of childhood, the process of data accumulation commences, and it continues unceasingly throughout the tapestry of our lives. Every significant interaction with our parents, teachers, society, and the vast spectrum of media amalgamates into a condensed vision, an illusionary portrayal intricately etched within the innermost layers of our mind. Additionally, retrieving information from a computer demands personal exertion, but the mind effortlessly brings out loads of data from its reservoirs, akin to an interest-free loan bestowed by a bank. As this perpetual cycle of input and output persists, the human being transforms into a mechanical contraption, brimming with complexities and reservations, unable to digest or halt the torrential flow of information spilling outward in the form of thoughts and dreams. We become hapless spectators, grappling to fathom the mechanisms that govern the mind—how our thoughts crystallise, and the significance and symbolism embedded within our dreams.

But just as we employ the principles of biology to comprehend the functioning of the human body, psychology serves as a valuable instrument to unravel the complex mechanisms of the human mind. While many perceive biology as a formidable realm, an even greater number find themselves entangled in the labyrinthine intricacies of psychology. It appears as a voyage into uncharted waters of the unmanifested mystical world, that only a few dauntlessly embark upon. And it is within this very exploration of the mind's mysteries that we discover how challenges can dissolve into opportunities and obstacles transform into pathways.

In this wondrous universe we inhabit, problems magically dissipate, giving way to an abundance of solutions. However arduous or bewildering a task may initially appear, once we set our minds and devote ourselves to it as a personal mission, a sublime harmony begins to unfurl. What once seemed insurmountable undergoes a transformation, becoming an attainable feat simply by taking that crucial first step.

Embarking upon a journey of the mind, though seemingly complicated, possesses relative simplicity. It is not an odyssey into the vast expanse of emptiness, but rather a sacred pilgrimage deep within oneself. In this divine realm, mystical visions flow abundantly, yearning for the gentle caress of love from the heart to the mind, unveiling the very essence of our existence and the profound truths of cosmic evolution.

To ensure that this voyage becomes a harmonious and enriching expedition, we shall delve into the complex workings of the mind, understanding its three distinct domains: the conscious, the unconscious, and the superconscious.

So, let us commence our exploration with the realm of the conscious, for it forms the foundational bedrock upon which we shall unravel the complexities that lie ahead. In truth, the study of the conscious mind mirrors the level of education one receives in high school, while the study of the unconscious mind aligns with the rigours of college, and the study of the superconscious mind embodies the lofty heights of university-level education. Just as our education commences within the hallowed halls of a school, we shall now consciously embark upon the realm of the conscious mind.

Chapter 1
The Conscious Mind

The Power of Creation Within

The essence of consciousness revolves around the profound awareness of right and wrong, permeating our actions and thoughts. It serves as the internal compass through which we gradually assess and ponder the morality of our deeds. Within the realm of the conscious mind, attempting to rationalise wrongdoing becomes a formidable feat.

The power of consciousness wields an extraordinary influence, transcending the boundaries of ordinary human comprehension. Regardless of the efforts one might exert, it distinguishes wrong from right with unflinching clarity, passing judgement untainted by bias. It could rightfully be dubbed the voice of divinity, casting an illuminating radiance of righteousness upon every action. No deed can be classified as virtuous or malevolent, motivated by love or enmity, until it undergoes the scrutiny of conscious examination, with utmost equanimity and unwavering awareness. This, indeed, stands as the sacred responsibility of the conscious mind.

Envision the transformative wave that would sweep across the world if our leaders embarked upon the journey of conscious leadership, steering their nations from darkness to light and their citizens from sorrow to elation. Imagine a life where our religious leaders consciously practice what they preach and become students before they teach. Picture a world where all those deemed leaders embrace a profound comprehension of consciousness, guided by a conscious mind. However, these aspirations often prove simpler to verbalise than to manifest. It is not due to a lack of endeavour that we stumble in overcoming our personal shortcomings and transcending the superficial dimensions of our humanity. We yearn for a life infused with virtue, robust well-being, boundless joy, resounding triumphs, and emancipation from ailments, medications, and afflictions. Yet have we genuinely ever disentangled a problem without delving into its underlying roots? The solutions frequently rest within arm's reach, even though they might initially appear distant. The elusive truth that eludes us is that our consciousness constitutes a mere ten per cent of the mind, while the remaining ninety per cent resides under the sway of the unconscious. This struggle between our aspirations and our actions points us to a deeper question about the mind itself, with its layers, its limits, and its unseen dominion over our choices.

This tension becomes evident in our everyday lives, surfacing in the small but telling moments when we act against our better judgement. How often do we recognise something as inherently wrong, yet still choose to ignore that inner voice and go ahead? Later, during moments of introspection, we lament our actions and vow that it shall be the last instance. Yet, how frequently have we faltered in upholding such solemn pledges? What facet of the mind whispers to us that our course is amiss? The answer lies in recognising that it is our diminutive but significant conscious mind, endowed with a paltry ten per cent power.

And the reason we persist, even while fully aware of the erroneous nature of our actions, lies in the dominance of the unconscious mind. With its ninety per cent control, it exercises complete governance over the conscious mind, influencing most of our deeds, conduct, inclinations, and aversions. It can be likened to a computer software program, orchestrating the intricate mechanisms of our psyche and propelling us towards distress and desolation, compelling us to partake in actions we would otherwise shun.

Consider, for instance, the scenario where you notice yourself gaining weight. A voice emanates from within, originating in your conscious mind, offering counsel to engage in physical exercise or modify your dietary preferences. Your conscious mind possesses the knowledge of the actions required to rectify the situation, yet, day after day, you find yourself perpetually postponing these steps, trapped in an unending cycle. Perhaps, eventually, you embark on a journey to the gym or alter your dietary habits, but before long, you surrender and return to the comforting routines of the past. A similar pattern unfolds when attempting to regulate or forsake any habits or behaviour perceived as detrimental to our well-being.

The important question here is: what truly drives such behaviour? What compels us to postpone decisions we sincerely aspire to, only to discard them with remarkable haste? While we might attribute it solely to our own volition, in truth, it is our unconscious mind—the predominant stakeholder within the realm of our mental landscape. Every predicament we encounter in life, whether physical or psychological, traces its origins in this profound disparity between our conscious and unconscious realms. This imbalance significantly reverberates through our well-being, vitality, and the very fabric of our relationships. This dynamic is analogous to the influence a mere ten per cent shareholder can wield in a corporation. Their role may be confined to voicing concerns and advocating for a brighter future during board meetings. However, the ultimate determinations that chart the company's trajectory rest in the hands of the individual overseeing the remaining ninety per cent of shares. Within the tapestry of human existence, the unconscious mind assumes a similar role to that of an influential and potent shareholder.

In most cases, people remain unaware of these essential truths and come to accept sickness, failure, and unhappiness as ordinary parts of life. However, illness should stand as a rare exception. We have every reason to anticipate continuous good health, liberation from pain, and a state of profound happiness. Yet, it is our lack of awareness of our true nature and limitless potential that forms the bedrock of human suffering. Our fundamental dilemma lies in our inclination to embrace falsehoods from all directions. We deceive ourselves into believing that good health, happiness, and wealth are privileges reserved exclusively for a chosen elite, erroneously excluding ourselves from their ranks. By succumbing to these lies, we inadvertently distance ourselves further from verity. We languish in sickness, unhappiness, and poverty, primarily because we have either accepted or resigned ourselves to this fallacy. In doing so, we lose touch with our conscious mind and the transformative power it holds—the power to transcend unconsciousness and reclaim our rightful status as sovereign beings rather than hapless beggars. It is therefore vital to recognise that within each of us lies an innate right to flourish and prosper. By tapping into our greatest endowment—

the power of creation—we can overcome the seemingly insurmountable and bring our dreams and aspirations to life. This empowerment eagerly awaits us once we wholeheartedly embrace the laws that govern our conscious nature.

Truth as the Key to Freedom

In the realm of deception, we often encounter a subtle yet powerful allure that holds sway over our perceptions and emotions. One iconic song from Fleetwood Mac, penned in the eighties, captures this sentiment perfectly, with its refrain asking: 'Tell me lies, tell me sweet little lies.' This hauntingly catchy melody speaks to the insidious nature of lies—the way they can be cloaked in sweetness, in comfort, in flattery, and yet ultimately, they always deceive. Undeniably, lies possess an almost saccharine allure, yet they unfailingly mislead, while the truth, though it may carry a bitter sting, remains steadfast in its authenticity. It is this unwavering nature of truth that ensures its eventual triumph over the fleeting nature of lies.

Consider a seemingly harmless scenario where someone compliments your appearance and praises your attire, and you, flattered, extend gratitude. At first glance, this exchange seems innocuous, perhaps even flattering. But underneath this well-meaning praise could lie something entirely different, a truth hidden from your view. In their thoughts, that individual might be ruminating, 'What an outlandish garment you are donning.' This thought, though unspoken, is their truth, a truth they have not shared with you. If they were to voice this thought, it might elicit anger, frustration, or even hurt. And so, the veil of the lie remains intact—one sweet little lie that shields the other person from the discomfort of expressing an unkind truth. In this instance, the lie functions as a kind of social lubricant, masking discomfort but distorting reality in the process.

An intriguing question arises here: what are these sweet little lies we tell ourselves, i.e., the illusions we create to shield us from the overwhelming truths of our existence? In the context of our vast mental landscape, the lies we tell ourselves are often the very beliefs that we cling to, the narratives we weave about our control over our lives and the world around us. It is an irrefutable truth that we, as conscious beings, are but a mere minority stakeholders in the grand scheme of our existence. The truth, however bitter it may be, reveals that we have no mastery over our lives. We deceive ourselves into believing that we are in charge, that we steer the course of our days, that we control our circumstances. Yet, in reality, the vast majority of our thoughts, actions, and decisions are dictated by our unconscious mind, which remains largely outside our conscious control. In fact, it is within this mysterious realm that the essence of who we are resides—our primal instincts, our deepest fears, and our true desires are held in this space, often beyond our immediate awareness.

This is the crux of the deception: we are not, in fact, the masters of our own destiny. Instead, we are servants to the unconscious forces that govern our behaviour, our relationships, and even our beliefs about ourselves. Day after day, we convince ourselves of the illusion of control, telling ourselves sweet little lies about our ability to shape our world. These lies provide comfort, a semblance of agency, but they ultimately keep us trapped in a state of ignorance, unaware of the vast forces that truly influence our lives. The unconscious mind, with its vast power and hidden influence, shapes the course of our lives, even as we cling to the illusion of autonomy and deny its hold on us. Put simply, we are, at our core, slaves to our unconscious minds. We exist under the sovereignty of these deeper mental forces, whether in an ignorant or ambitious state, regardless of our choice to acknowledge them. Yet, it is only by confronting this truth, by accepting the limitations of our conscious mind and recognising the vast power of the unconscious, that we can begin to free ourselves.

As a sage of yore proclaimed, 'Truth is freedom.' These words, spoken centuries ago, resonate as powerfully today as they did in the past. Truth, in its purest form, is the key to liberation. It may be uncomfortable, even painful, to confront the reality of our limited control, but it is only through this confrontation that we can begin to break free from the chains of self-deception. The truth, once embraced, has the power to dissolve the illusions that bind us. And no matter how sweet the lie, it cannot conceal the force of truth.

In the end, it is the truth that leads us to true freedom, to an authentic life lived in harmony with the forces that shape us. Only by shedding the little lies we tell ourselves can we begin to align with the deeper truths within and around us. These truths, when accepted, hold the power to set us free, for truth is an enduring force that transcends time itself.

Chapter 2
The Unconscious Mind

The Shadowed Realm of Slumber

The term 'unconscious' represents a complete absence of awareness of our actions and words, akin to being in a slumber or trance-like state, where the ability to discern right from wrong has been relinquished. It carries a literal meaning, denoting that aspect of our mental activity which remains beyond our conscious awareness. However, it can be unraveled and comprehended through the skilled analysis of dreams, behaviour, or hypnotism.

Many sages and mystics would often impart such words to their devoted disciples: 'Awake and be vigilant, for if the master of the house had known when the thief would come, he would have kept watch and prevented his home from being broken into.' Expanding on these parables, they would add, 'Therefore, I speak to them in parables, for though they possess the faculty of sight, they do not truly perceive, and though they possess the faculty of hearing, they do not truly listen or understand.' What profound message did they strive to convey through these seemingly simple yet enigmatic words? Were they merely urging their disciples to awaken from spiritual slumber, or did these teachings hold a deeper, hidden significance?

Throughout the tapestry of history, parables and teachings from eminent sages and sacred scriptures have suffered from gross misinterpretation, for though we possess the ability to see, we often fail to truly perceive, and though we possess the ability to hear, we often fail to genuinely listen or comprehend. Most individuals, groups, and sects have molded these teachings to suit their particular circumstances, aligning them with the inclinations of their unconscious minds. Consequently, the authentic essence of the messages and teachings imparted by figures such as Buddha, Jesus, Muhammad, Guru Nanak, and other spiritual luminaries has regrettably faded into the recesses of obscurity.

Coming back to our earlier question, these wake-up calls can indeed be seen as a direct allusion to the disciples' inner state—their unconscious slumber and the condition of their minds. The 'master' of the house may be understood as the conscious self, while the 'thief' symbolises intrusive, unchecked thoughts that stealthily shape our lives. In simpler terms, these teachings are reminders to be mindful of every single thought. Whether good or bad, our thoughts inevitably shape our actions, leading us along paths of triumph or defeat, elation or despair. The power of choice eternally resides within us, and it is our sacred prerogative to consciously select our course through contemplation, exploration, and introspection, reaping the corresponding rewards.

Another story that captures the deep-rooted patterns of the unconscious mind is that of a wealthy man preparing to embark on an extended journey. Prior to his departure, he admonished his loyal servants, 'Remain ever vigilant, safeguard, and tend to my abode, for I may return unannounced at any given moment. Should I discover you enveloped in slumber, your esteemed positions shall be forfeited. Given your multitude, divide your responsibilities wisely, ensuring a constant watch is maintained.'

Once the master embarked on his sojourn, the servants, under the misguided assumption that his return would be distant, reveled in merriment and succumbed to the embrace of slumber throughout the initial year. After all, their master was away and a liberating sensation of unbridled freedom coursed through their veins. The passage of time saw the master's absence stretch into a second year, yet the servants persisted in their indulgences. Gradually, the memory of their master's exhortation to remain ever awake and alert faded, as they continuously postponed the implementation of his counsel day after day.

Ultimately, after the passage of three long years, the master made his triumphant return, only to discover his servants mired in the depths of indolence. When one spends a prolonged period immersed in slumber and idle pursuits, lethargy inevitably takes hold. The extended absence of their master led the servants to assume, 'He shall never grace us with his presence again; who knows whether he walks among the living or has transcended beyond? Why bother adhering to his instructions? Why stay constantly watchful and alert?' Not only had they forsaken their master's directives, but as the once-pristine abode descended into a state of disarray, the servants even forgot their designated role and began to perceive themselves as masters. Lost within an eternal slumber, they remained oblivious to the truth, wholly unconscious of their own identities.

Reflecting upon this mystical narrative, it becomes imperative to grasp the origins and intricate manifestations of the unconscious mind, delving deeply into its complex genesis. Nestled within our very core, it takes root, nurtured by primordial patterns inherited from our primal instincts and the fundamental need to endure within the captivating tapestry of human existence. Moreover, the unconsciousness constitutes a reservoir of profound depths, an amalgamation of our past lives and innate nature, encompassing the entirety of our evolutionary odyssey—a testament to all that we were prior to our present incarnation. To better understand this hidden force, we must trace its beginnings, observing how it first takes shape at the very dawn of human life.

The moment a child emerges into the world, a new chapter unfurls within the realm of the unconscious, commencing the instant they depart the sanctuary of their mother's womb. Swathed in the comforting embrace of darkness, the child finds solace and security for nine lunar cycles, sheltered from the perils that lie beyond. Yet, as they emerge from this cocoon of tranquility and are abruptly thrust into the blinding radiance of light, an intense jolt reverberates through their being—an awakening shock. No longer bound by the confines of their parental haven, the child must navigate, survive, and flourish in this foreign realm, as the unconsciousness within them seeks to adapt, survive, and thrive in its own enigmatic ways.

Within the realm of our existence on earth, cycles govern the processes of survival and growth, commencing from the moment of birth and recurring in rhythmic patterns. The earth itself gracefully rotates on its axis, tracing a path from the west to the east, encapsulating a span of twenty-four hours—the ebb and flow of day and night. Furthermore, it orbits the radiant sun, completing three hundred and sixty-five days, giving rise to the ever-shifting tapestry of seasons. Yet, beyond these celestial rhythms, a mystical number, seven, weaves its intricate dance, leaving its indelible mark on our lives.

Firstly, we are bestowed with seven bodies—the physical, etheric, astral, mental, spiritual, cosmic, and nirvanic—each holding profound significance within its unique domain. Even within the physical realm, a weekly cycle unfolds, composed of seven days, mirroring the harmonious progression of the seven musical notes within an octave. Secondly, our corporeal vessel harbors seven chakras, intricately interwoven energy centres that govern various facets of our being. These chakras—the root, sacral, solar plexus, heart, throat, third eye, and crown—each resonating with a specific body, undergo cycles of activation and growth every seven years, as our transformative journey unfolds. Most importantly, during the initial seven years, the tapestry of our physical body and the enigmatic unconscious mind unfurls, ignited by the awakening of the dormant root chakra—a profound moment that breathes life into our very being.

From the tender age of eight to fourteen, a delicate metamorphosis takes hold—an exquisite blossoming of our etheric body, revealing the intricacies of emotions and the stirring currents of burgeoning sexuality. At this juncture, the vibrant sacral chakra stirs to life, infusing our existence with newfound vigor and vibrancy. And as the subsequent seven-year cycle dawns, spanning from fifteen to twenty-one, the ethereal veil of the astral body takes shape, accompanied by the emergence of heightened thinking, sharpened intellect, and the blossoming of reason's delicate petals. It is a profound epoch, wherein the radiant solar plexus chakra awakens, casting its luminous glow upon the path we tread.

The fourth cycle of seven years, from twenty-two to twenty-eight, marks a pivotal ascent—the rise of the mental body, wherein realms of imagination and dreams unfurl their majestic wings. It is a time of fleeting glimpses into our latent powers, guided by the awakened symphony of the heart chakra. As the journey of growth continues beyond this phase, a deeper awakening stirs, preparing the ground for the blossoming of the spiritual body.

From age twenty-nine to thirty-five, the seeds of the spiritual body begin to sprout, beckoning profound inquiries into the mysteries of birth, death, religion, and the divine. Within this sacred phase, the enigmatic throat chakra unfurls its delicate petals, granting voice to our innermost contemplations. The subsequent seven-year span, spanning from thirty-six to forty-two, bears witness to the maturation of the cosmic body. Having traversed the realms of spiritual growth through the preceding seven-year cycle, this phase propels us further, guiding us to discern our true purpose in life and uncover the veiled reservoirs of hidden powers. It is within this sacred juncture that the third eye chakra, the seat of intuition, awakens, illuminating hidden pathways of perception.

Finally, the culmination of this wondrous odyssey arrives with the development of the nirvanic body, from age forty-three to forty-nine. As the majestic crown chakra activates, the ethereal realm of nirvana unfolds—a transcendent state of ultimate realisation, where enlightenment, awakening, salvation, and emancipation from the eternal cycles of birth and death converge. It stands as the pinnacle of superconsciousness, a divine tapestry woven with threads of boundless wisdom and serenity.

Yet, amidst this natural activation cycle of the seven chakras and the development of the seven bodies, a striking reality reveals itself: nearly eighty per cent of humankind, deeply entwined within the clutches of unconsciousness, never transcend beyond the realm of the fourth body. Up until this stage, their journey remains entangled in the materialistic realm, finding contentment solely in external aspects of existence. The threshold of the fifth body, which opens the gates to the spiritual realm, appears treacherous and shrouded in fear. The mere contemplation of mortality sends shivers down our spines, and venturing into the uncharted territories of the senses seems an intimidating expedition. Hence, only a select few dare to venture beyond the confines of the fourth body, embarking upon a sacred quest that unravels the extraordinary, supernatural powers inherent within the depths of the human spirit.

The Seven-Year Imprint

As we delve deeper into the mystical realm of the unconscious mind's development, let's retrace our steps and explore its transformative journey. From our earlier discussion, it is within the tender embrace of the first seven years of childhood, when the dormant root chakra stirs to life, that the foundation for the physical body takes shape. This pivotal period marks the genesis of our initial learning, the awakening of our senses—taste, sound, touch—and the delicate emergence of emotions, love, and all that encompasses our being.

During this extraordinary phase, our innate survival instincts and primal nature intertwine, birthing a complex, computerised programme that will shape our entire life, governing each facet of our behaviour. As this vital programme takes shape, the child's unconscious mind deftly absorbs every significant habit exhibited by their parents or those in their immediate environment, assimilating their mode of interaction both within the familial abode and the expansive material world.

Now let's look at the following question: Why do children, as they mature, often mirror the behaviours of their parents? The scientific explanation lies within the realm of genetic coding, a testament to the multifaceted nature of truth. Yet, truth, much like a coin, reveals two sides that ultimately converge upon the same core essence. In the same vein, an alternate truth emerges, positing that the programme formed within the unconscious mind during the formative years of the initial seven-year cycle is responsible for the lifelong mirroring of parental behaviour. Undoubtedly, genetic factors hold sway, particularly in matters pertaining to the physical realm. For instance, a diabetic or asthmatic parent may bestow upon their children the genetic predisposition for such conditions. However, the realm of the mind exists as an autonomous domain, untouched by the transference of genes, transcending the confines of the physical body. It thrives as an ethereal entity, interconnected with the human spirit, impervious to genetic inheritance.

This is due to the fact that by the age of seven, the unconscious mind blossoms into a fully realised entity—an inner child that endures throughout one's life, unless the adult embarks upon a profound voyage of transformation to alter the prevailing web of childhood conditioning. While the journey of learning continues unabated, the growth of the unconscious mind finds its culmination within this threshold. The primary programme has been intricately woven and installed, shaped by the child's experiences and observations during these formative years.

The inner child, having traversed the stages of growth, now stands prepared to influence and play games with you for the rest of your life.

To grasp the weight of this influence, we must turn to the question of what exactly the child has absorbed during these tender years. In every incarnation of our learning journey on earth, the situation and environment within the home lay the foundational bedrock and stepping-stone for every child. It is within this hallowed familial institution that the nascent roots of a child's unconscious mind are nurtured, influenced predominantly by the interactions and acts of the mother and father.

Observe any typical married couple and note the intricate tapestry of their daily lives; you will discern their distinct preferences, aversions, opinions, and behavioural patterns. Ask them about the essence of marriage and the motives behind their sacred union, and the responses will invariably echo the same refrain: 'Because everybody eventually gets married.' Likewise, if you inquire about their desire to have children, the answer will resonate similarly, 'Because everyone has children.' Cease further questioning, for the answers shall remain indistinguishable. When responses align regarding the two most cardinal aspects of human existence—marriage and children—pillars upon which the foundation of humanity stands, what divergent answers can one anticipate regarding life's fleeting details? More importantly, from where do these answers truly emanate?

Enveloped within the vast realm of unconsciousness, such responses arise as a wellspring from the depths of our unconscious minds, where the predominant ninety per cent of our mental realm holds dominion. This prompts another query: what underlies this phenomenon? The response lies in our possession of at least ten per cent consciousness, wherein the seed of absolute potentiality is deeply embedded within the very essence of human nature.

This hierarchy of consciousness reverberates throughout the natural world; trees exude a more intricate consciousness than rocks, animals manifest a higher level of consciousness than trees, and humankind outshines animals in their expansive conscious awareness. As humanity stands as the culmination of evolutionary progress, it becomes indispensable to comprehend the true essence of evolution. Is it merely the transition from animal to human form, or rather, the voyage from the slumber of unconsciousness to the awakening of heightened consciousness? This is the very journey that Buddha, Jesus, Muhammad, and Guru Nanak embarked upon, transcending the confines of ordinary existence through resolute efforts, fully harnessing the seeds of consciousness to diminish the realm of unconsciousness. Meanwhile, within us, these seeds remain dormant, awaiting the nurturing touch of cultivation.

Beyond Tradition: The True Essence of Marriage

For deeper introspection into the labyrinthine corridors of the unconscious mind, it becomes imperative to fathom the true essence of marriage through the clarifying lens of conscious awareness. From the time of Adam and Eve, the relationship between parents has played a role of paramount significance in shaping the growth and evolution of a child's unconscious mind. Allow me, therefore, to poetically illumine the authentic essence of marriage.

Marriage, a sacred union on terrestrial terrain,
Where body entwines with body,
Heart melds with heart,
And soul converges with soul.
Marriage, a lifelong odyssey,
Of give and take,
As two hearts embrace each other,
Face to face.
Marriage, a fusion of sugar and honey,
Blended into an exotic elixir,
The more love you infuse,
The sweeter the taste.
Marriage, magic moments of enchantment shared,
In the divine symphony of existence,
When two lovebirds weave their hearts,
With mystical threads of trust and faith.
Marriage, a realisation that the earthly union of souls,
Merely heralds the dawning,
Of a grander reunion,
With the supreme soul.

Marriage stands as an exquisite bond where two hearts and souls converge, rekindling their essence and intertwining with cosmic evolution. Why is man drawn to woman and woman to man? It is because they are two halves of a whole, indivisible and interwoven. As ancient scriptures narrate, Eve was sculpted from Adam's rib, fashioned to be his companion. What lies beneath the surface of this tale? Could it be that Eve was not merely moulded from Adam's rib, but that God endowed her with a fragment of his soul? Thus, man ceaselessly seeks the missing portion of his being in a woman, and the woman seeks her counterpart; they embark on a quest to reunite with the piece from which they originated. Both are driven by an unyielding quest, for they are incomplete without one another. This inherent yearning and attraction lay the cornerstone of their initial connection, and marriage serves as the inception of their wondrous voyage of self-discovery.

How many of us truly embrace this simple reality of life and the profound truth behind our creation? As unconsciousness reigns supreme within our inner dominion, marriage, like many other facets of existence, has been reduced to a mere tradition—an entity devoid of life, a betrayal of life itself. Intriguingly, the words tradition and traitor share the first three letters, and their link runs deeper than linguistic coincidence. A traitor betrays, and indeed, traditions have been betraying us, for they stand in contradiction to life's essence. Life, akin to a flowing river, moves ceaselessly, altering its course with every passing moment. You can never step into the same river twice, or even once, as its waters perpetually shift. Try immersing your feet in a river and observe the water that touches you. You will notice that, like life, water is in constant motion—never stagnant—as new currents continually replace the old in rhythmic succession. Even our very cells undergo constant evolution, as new ones replace the old, a dynamic flux mirroring the river's flow. Moreover, nature itself is a manifestation of continuous change—the trees, plants, and flowers you behold in the morning undergo transformation by noon. The rosebud, kissed by the early morning sun, gradually unfurls throughout the day, a poetic dance choreographed by warmth and light.

Similarly, marriage, like that rosebud, holds the potential for partners to open their hearts, unfold their inner selves, and blossom with the boundless love of the cosmos, merging their souls into a harmonious symphony. Regrettably, the reality is that ninety per cent of marriages have devolved into mere traditions, and just as traditions betray, so do married couples—not each other, but themselves. Like any tradition, modern-day marriages come burdened with preconceived conditions, fixed laws, and obligations that each partner must adhere to. They have transmuted into professional partnerships, devoid of emotional resonance. Love, in its true essence, has been vanquished, replaced by self-serving motives and a transactional mindset. Each partner exploits the other for personal gratification, reducing every interaction to a materialistic exchange. As our lives advance in the realm of scientific innovation, the true meaning of love has become obscured. Life has shifted its focus towards material pursuits, and marriages have become ensnared in the web of materialistic traditions.

Thus, it is crucial to understand the immense significance of marriage as it serves as the pivotal force sculpting the intricate tapestry of a child's unconscious mind. In the formative years, spanning from birth to age seven, the home environment unfolds as the canvas upon which the strokes of a child's future are painted. Their mind meticulously captures even the most inconspicuous details—the dynamics of the parents' relationship, their interactions with extended family, friends, and more. As parents unconsciously engage in their actions, the child's unconscious mind diligently registers these acts, akin to a computer programme being encoded. By the age of seven, this programme is poised to operate as the child's lifelong companion, exerting substantial influence over their mental landscape, behavioural traits, and relationships. Moreover, children mirror not just the words and actions of their parents, but also the unspoken thoughts that linger within their parents' minds. At times, it can be quite startling to witness how faithfully a child echoes or articulates our very own opinions and reflections.

Hence, during this period, a harmonious and nurturing ambience, coupled with a loving relationship between parents, acts as fertile soil for the positive germination of the seeds of unconscious impressions. Conversely, an environment tainted by discord and a love-hate dynamic steeped in materialism, can direct the trajectory of the child's unconscious mind towards negativity. This is especially true in our contemporary era, where many parents appear to falter in grasping the genuine meaning of love, giving, sharing, caring, and forgiving. Authenticity and sincerity seem to elude this pivotal relationship, as their comprehension remains confined within the narrow boundaries of tradition, overshadowed by a desire to manipulate situations to their advantage. Genuine marriages rooted in unconditional love between parents seem to be glaringly absent from existence. Instead, a veneer of falsity and unreality prevails, inundating the child's nascent unconscious mind with a torrent of negativity.

Silently, the child observes it all, as the unconscious behaviours, thoughts, and actions of their parents imprint themselves upon the child's burgeoning unconscious mind. Gradually, the programme takes shape, destined to guide their entire lifetime.

The irony here is that most parents yearn for their children to emulate their ways and even grow up swiftly, and in due course, these aspirations are realised. The children indeed become reflections of their parents, maturing at an accelerated pace. Yet, more often than not, parents find themselves discontented with the outcomes, as reality fails to align with the idealised images they had envisioned. Unbeknownst to us, our unconscious mind exerts a potent sway over our every action, and the children, astute observers, internalise those very actions, mirroring our behaviour and adopting our attitudes as their own. It is the shadowy aspect of our nature, a facet many are reluctant to acknowledge, let alone accept.

So, what is the solution? As mentioned earlier, a child possesses an extraordinary ability to learn, emulate, and internalise the unconscious behaviour and habits of adults with astonishing precision. There is no necessity for explicit teachings, lectures, or coercive imposition upon our children concerning how they ought to conduct themselves. Instead, we must embody the qualities and virtues we aspire for them to embrace, leading by personal example that far surpasses any formal instruction. If we yearn to quell their anger, we must first conquer our own. If we seek their obedience, we must exemplify heightened obedience to our conscious mind. If we perceive a lack of concentration in them, we must turn our focus inward to the workings of our own unconscious mind.

Honouring the Sacred Bond

The pressing need of our era is to restore the sanctity of the sacred bond of marriage and nurture it to thrive. By unconditionally bestowing boundless love and respect upon your partner and sowing the seeds of giving, you will inevitably reap the rewards in due time. When harvest time arrives, the abundance of fruits will surpass your expectations, much beyond the seeds you have sown. And much like how you reminisce about the enchanting moments of your child's birth and growth as you celebrate their tenth or fifteenth birthday, a wedding anniversary should evoke a similar sentiment. It is an occasion to traverse memory lanes, not merely to recollect but also to recreate some of those enchanting moments once again. It would not be out of place for married couples to take a brief respite, embarking on a mini-honeymoon for each anniversary. Such interludes would afford them the time to contemplate, explore, and reflect on their marriage, relive cherished moments, recognise where they may have faltered, and return to their daily lives as rejuvenated, reborn soulmates.

Grasping the true meaning of marriage will also pave the way to greater consciousness, as it marks the beginning of a transformative journey to revisit and rekindle the core essence of our marital bond. When two partners enter into marriage, it is akin to two rivers flowing in different directions. Although their paths may diverge, their ultimate destination remains constant—to merge into the vast ocean of boundless love and become a singular entity.

All in all, marriage stands as a transformative instrument, meticulously crafted to awaken our consciousness and teach us the art of harmonious co-existence and unconditional love for one another. And to honour marriage is to honour the very fabric of life. This calls us to seek a deeper understanding and reconnection with the profound truth at the heart of these sacred bonds.

The Imprint of Religion on the Unconscious Mind

As we look deeper into the roots of the unconscious mind, it becomes clear that a child does not grow in isolation but is profoundly shaped by the environment around them.

An important point to consider is that parental behaviour and thoughts not only influence a child's unconscious programming, but their personal convictions, insecurities, habits, and fears also leave a lasting imprint. Among these influences, religious beliefs hold a particular prominence. A closer analysis will help us understand this better.

It is commonplace for individuals to grapple with a sense of dissatisfaction with their parental upbringing, often perceiving a disconnect within the eternal bond of kinship. What factors contribute to this prevailing disconnection? A deeper introspection reveals that the unease often arises from a profound discord with the beliefs, fears, religious conditioning, traditions, and habits inherited from one's parents. These elements, deeply ingrained in the unconscious mind, now wield significant influence over our lives, rendering personal transformation a daunting task. Yet, the underlying truth remains steadfast: the conditioning and upbringing bestowed upon us were unwittingly inherited from the unconscious minds of our parents, who in turn received the same from their ancestors—a perpetual tapestry woven throughout our evolutionary journey on earth.

Undoubtedly, there exists a pivotal juncture in time and space, from which this intriguing web of existence originated. And when we embark on a journey to unearth its roots, we will find ourselves unable to transcend beyond the establishment of world religions, as these deeply rooted unconscious patterns and ingrained habits are inherently intertwined with our religious conditioning. From the very day of birth, a child is labelled and confined to a predetermined trajectory. Whether born into a Hindu family, a Christian family, or a Muslim family, the child inevitably inherits the corresponding identity. This demarcation of the mind and the inception of the unconscious begins from the moment of birth.

The Hindu child matures under the influence of Hindu conditioning, embracing diverse beliefs and practices. Similarly, the Christian child adheres to Christian conditioning, and even within this realm, divisions arise—Catholic, Protestant, and the like. Likewise, the Muslim child follows Muslim conditioning, encountering divisions of its own—Shia, Sunni, and beyond.

Religions, therefore, have inadvertently contributed to the fragmentation of humankind rather than its unity, contradicting the very purpose for which they came into being. Each proclaims its superiority over the others, extolling its founders as God's chosen progeny, prophets, or messiahs. Yet, they overlook the undeniable truth that none of them created these so-called religions.

In reality, the collective goal of all religions was to dissolve existing divisions, to unveil the essence of love, and to rouse us from our unconscious slumber into heightened consciousness. However, the followers took divergent paths, fanning the flames of divisions by erecting more barriers and giving rise to additional religions in their name. These divisions continue unabated, with our small world now hosting over four thousand religions, encompassing major world religions, indigenous traditions, and various sects and denominations within larger faiths.

The word 'religion' traces its roots back to the Latin term 'religere,' fundamentally signifying a reunion with oneself and the cosmos. But why does this need for reunion arise? It is because our conscious and unconscious minds have drifted far apart. Despite being integral facets of a unified whole, an intense schism has emerged, estranging them from each other. The authentic essence of religion, as espoused by Buddha, Jesus, Muhammad, and Guru Nanak, lies in reuniting these two realms, recognising them as inseparable components of our authentic self, our soul or spirit. Only when these two forces of the mind blend harmoniously can we entertain the possibility of reconnecting with ourselves and the vast cosmos.

Yet, do individuals around the globe truly grasp the genuine meaning of religion? The prevailing understanding often manifests as identifying oneself primarily as a Buddhist, Christian, Muslim, Hindu, or Sikh. One's birth determines one's religious affiliation, allowing no room for free choice or independent will. Paradoxically, despite our fervent discourse on democracy and the freedom of speech, faith, and thought, our children frequently find themselves living under a form of subtle dictatorship as we unconsciously impose our religious beliefs, traditions, and customs on them. In this context, a captivating tale emerges, derived from an ancient narrative but tailored to suit our contemporary times, eloquently illustrating our current life scenario.

Once upon a time, there lived a man who had sustained a leg injury. Following his doctor's counsel, he employed a crutch to aid his mobility for a span of weeks until his leg was fully restored. As time went by, his leg recuperated, but the man had grown accustomed to the presence of the crutch. Its utility extended beyond its intended purpose; it became a versatile tool—a defense against stray dogs during walks or serving as a protective weapon if needed. The advantages seemed endless.

Excitedly, the man shared his newfound knowledge with his family, and they too embraced the use of crutches when they walked. The word of this intriguing discovery swiftly spread among the neighbours, and when they inquired, they too were enlightened about the benefits of walking with crutches.

As the grass appears greener on the other side, the entire community enthusiastically embraced this practice. Before long, the phenomenon reached the town, prompting even more individuals to incorporate crutches into their daily routine. The crutch-selling business flourished, resulting in shops sprouting up across the landscape. Manufacturers, eager to cater to varying preferences and budgets, began crafting an array of crutches—some fashioned from durable metals, others graced with opulent gold or ivory handles, and even those bedecked with glistening diamonds.

As time marched forward, brand names emerged, and designer crutches became the talk of the town. Youngsters proudly showcased their elegantly designed crutches, while the older generation stuck to their tried-and-true wooden versions, often lamenting the wastefulness of the younger brigade's obsession with extravagant designer crutches.

The possession of the latest, most expensive crutch soon became a marker of social status. Lavish sets of crutches became customary gifts, reserved for occasions ranging from birthdays to weddings and anniversaries. At parties or social gatherings, everyone proudly displayed their prized possessions—a gold, ivory, bronze, or designer crutch. Walking with crutches evolved into an established tradition, with children being taught to wield them from infancy.

Years flowed by, and eventually, some individuals began to question their reliance on crutches, realising they were no longer indispensable. However, this audacious act was deemed scandalous and a violation of societal norms and traditions. The younger generation, especially, faced random arrests for challenging the established behaviour, and their release was conditional upon attending classes that extolled the virtues of walking with crutches.

Gradually, more influential figures joined the ranks of those questioning the necessity of crutches, as they recognised that these aids were no longer prerequisites for walking. Yet, they faced severe criticism and backlash for attempting to dismantle a tradition the town had meticulously built. Business magnates and manufacturers vehemently opposed this growing movement, fearing a significant decline in sales. They were reluctant to let go of a lucrative enterprise, second only to the food industry.

In response, the business and religious leaders initiated a concerted campaign to halt the spread of crutch-less walking. They drew upon scriptural passages to sway public opinion, contending that a crutch was indeed an indispensable tool. For instance, they referenced the words of a renowned sage who had proclaimed, 'Man cannot live by bread alone.' They argued that, undoubtedly, a crutch was just as essential as bread—a vital instrument for work, sustenance, family provision, and safeguarding one's earnings.

This instance is a recurring theme. How often do we witness the teachings of scripture being misconstrued by some misguided and unconscious individuals? That sage had merely illuminated a simple verity: while bread sustains a person physically, they require something more—a means to awaken their true being, nourishment for the soul that steers them out of unconsciousness into a conscious world.

Throughout the annals of time, humanity at large has relied on metaphorical crutches to navigate the winding journey of life. Wise sages and spiritual luminaries—Buddha,

Jesus, Muhammad, and Guru Nanak—walked among us, propelled by a mission to rouse our slumbering unconscious minds. They sought to remove the crutches we clung to, shedding light upon our stumbles, and illuminating the true essence of religion. Their teachings conveyed that religion is not a mere crutch, tradition, or organisation, but rather akin to a flowing river—an eternal stream that descends ceaselessly from lofty peaks, cascading like a resplendent waterfall. Along its course, this river tenderly nurtures fields, cultivating empathy and understanding, bolstering human well-being, until it harmoniously merges with the boundless ocean of infinite love.

Therefore, it is vital to understand that religion is not an inherent birthright; true spirituality must be cultivated within oneself. The seeds of spiritual awakening lie dormant within each of us, awaiting the opportunity to sprout and blossom. If one dares to peer deep into the recesses of their unconscious mind with the radiant light of consciousness, they will come to realise that the prevalent religions of the modern world are mere sects and traditions. And when consciousness illuminates the unconscious, religion gives way to realisation, and tradition yields to truth. That is the essence of genuine spirituality.

Chapter 3

THE SUPERCONSCIOUS MIND

The Pinnacle of Awakening

SUPERCONSCIOUSNESS SIGNIFIES A REALM OF AWARENESS that transcends the confines of ordinary human perception, elevating individuals to possess heightened strength, capacity, awareness, and intelligence. In numerous facets, it draws parallels with the extraordinary capabilities of Superman, empowering individuals to achieve feats that lie far beyond the grasp of the common man. Put simply, it stands as the pinnacle of transformation, uplifting an ordinary person and propelling them into the realm of the truly extraordinary.

As discussed earlier, to be unconscious is to remain in a deep slumber, disconnected from the world around us. Being conscious, on the other hand, implies being awake and aware of our surroundings, thoughts, and emotions. Yet, even in consciousness, we may find ourselves not entirely in command of the unfolding of our internal and external experiences. It is in the emergence of superconsciousness that a magical metamorphosis occurs, becoming the transformative threshold between the realms of unconsciousness and consciousness. In this transcendent state, individuals are liberated from the chains of the past and the anxieties of the future and ushered into the sacred realm of the present moment—an ethereal domain of everlasting bliss.

Within this exalted state, one transcends the limitations of mere humanity, experiencing a sublime reunion with the divine essence, the soul or spirit. This state of supreme awakening is often denoted as enlightenment, and it has been attained by luminaries throughout history, including Buddha, Jesus, Muhammad, Guru Nanak, and an array of other remarkable souls. It is imperative to grasp that these enlightened beings were not inherently born enlightened. Instead, they entered the world just like any other human, carrying within them the seeds and latent potential to transcend the boundaries of ordinary existence. Through their profound inner work and resolute dedication, they cultivated the power to surmount every obstacle and ascend to the elevated plane of superconsciousness.

The journey of Buddha towards spiritual ascension is one that has been extensively documented, offering valuable insights to help us discover our individual paths towards enlightenment. Born in 560 BC into a prosperous kingdom, Siddhartha Gautama, as he was named, lived a life of luxury and abundance. However, around the age of twenty-nine, he became acutely aware of the stark contrast between his opulent lifestyle and the grave suffering endured by people around him. This realisation ignited a deep sense of compassion and an insatiable desire to fathom the roots of human suffering. He therefore embarked on a transformative quest for spiritual understanding, abandoning his palace and princely status. For years, he immersed himself in ascetic practices, seeking wisdom through encounters with philosophers and scholars, and subjecting himself to rigorous meditative techniques and austere forest living.

At the age of thirty-five, he recognised that these arduous practices did not lead him closer to the truth he sought.

Shifting course, he emphasised the middle way—a path that balanced the conscious and unconscious forces of the mind—placing greater emphasis on meditation. It was through this shift that he attained complete awakening or enlightenment and spent the remaining forty-five years of his life sharing his revelations. He fervently proclaimed that he was not a special individual or a chosen messenger of God, and that enlightenment was not an otherworldly phenomenon. Rather, it was the result of diligently attending to the nature of the human mind, attainable by any individual.

Although Jesus and Muhammad emerged centuries after Buddha, the precise details of their journeys towards enlightenment and the attainment of superconsciousness are not as extensively documented. Many of their followers generally perceive them as chosen messengers of God, entrusted with delivering divine teachings. However, seeking objective facts can shed light on this enigmatic subject and allow for a deeper understanding of their spiritual quests.

Muhammad, born in 570 AD, bore the burden of losing his father before his birth and his mother when he was just five years old. During his formative years, he found solace and purpose under the guardianship of his uncle, whom he assisted in tending and caring for a flock of sheep. With unwavering love and devotion, he nurtured the flock, honing his compassion and nurturing spirit.

At the age of twenty, Muhammad's heart was stirred by the plight of the downtrodden and oppressed. He joined a society dedicated to uplifting the poor and championing justice, becoming an advocate for those whose voices were stifled by the weight of inequality. He immersed himself in this noble pursuit, driven by a deep sense of empathy and a burning desire to create a more just and equitable society.

At twenty-five, Muhammad entered the sacred realms of matrimony with a woman of wealth and experience, who was a widow and fifteen years his senior. This union not only united their lives but also opened doors to new horizons. He assumed command of his wife's caravans and embarked on commercial journeys that took him to the bustling markets of Syria and the exotic lands of Yemen. It was during these travels that he honed his astute business acumen, acquiring knowledge and expanding his perspective on the diverse tapestry of humanity. Through his resolute dedication and unblemished integrity, the epithet *al-amin,* meaning 'the trustworthy,' became synonymous with his name. The news about his noble character spread far and wide, earning him respect and admiration from friends and foes alike.

However, it was when he reached the age of forty-two in 612 AD that a profound transformation engulfed his entire being. Seeking solace and guidance, he turned to the seclusion of a tranquil cave on Mount Hira—a sacred refuge nestled near Mecca, where he would immerse himself in deep devotion for extended periods.

After briefly returning home to replenish provisions, he would invariably find himself irresistibly drawn back to the sanctity of this divine cave. It was within this hallowed sanctuary that the truth of existence finally illuminated his being, unfurling with majestic splendor and breathtaking wonder. This pivotal moment marked his awakening, his enlightenment—a spiritual experience akin to the enlightenment of Buddha.

From that transformative encounter onward, for the next two decades until his earthly departure, he embarked on a tireless mission, preaching the divine message of Allah or God. His noble aim was to alleviate the sufferings of humanity and guide them steadfastly towards the path of righteousness.

Jesus, born about 560 years after Buddha, shared a similar disillusionment with the state of humanity's unconsciousness and the self-inflicted suffering plaguing the world. While the Bible provides glimpses into his birth and early childhood, including the notable account of his visit to the temple at the tender age of twelve, there remains a significant gap in the recorded history of his life, spanning the subsequent eighteen years.

It is intriguing to ponder why the earlier years are chronicled while the following period remains shrouded in mystery. Could there be a deliberate effort to conceal the truth, preserving his well-publicised image as a supernatural figure—the chosen one, the special messenger, the son of God believed to have been born enlightened? The truth, however, unveils a divine journey of self-discovery and inner exploration undertaken by Jesus during those unrecorded years. Driven by an insatiable quest and a profound desire to heal his fellow human beings and awaken them from their deep unconscious slumber, he embarked on extensive travels and immersed himself in the study of Jewish, Hindu, and Buddhist scriptures. His remarkable teachings included quotes from the Old Testament, the Upanishads, and the Bhagavad Gita, albeit with his own distinctive interpretations.

Jesus diverged from the conventional 'eye for an eye and tooth for a tooth' ethos, propounding revolutionary concepts like 'love your enemy' and 'turn the other cheek.' These ideas resonated profoundly with the teachings of Buddha. Both these spiritual giants radiated boundless love and compassion for humanity, earnestly seeking avenues to alleviate suffering and foster greater harmony.

Historical trails suggest Jesus voyaged to the far East, encompassing visits to Tibet, the Himalayas, and India during his enigmatic missing years. Russian novelist Nicolas Notovitch, in his illuminating tome *The Unknown Life of Jesus Christ,* attested to discovering a manuscript in Tibet detailing Jesus' sojourn. Other works, including *A Search for the Historical Jesus* by Fida Hassnain, *Jesus Lived in India* by Holger Kersten, and *The Autobiography of Jesus of Nazareth and the Missing Years* by Richard G. Patton, chronicle his odyssey to India. Within the intricate weave of these narratives, it is unveiled that Jesus, akin to Buddha, sought the company of spiritual luminaries, philosophers, and scholars. In these assemblies, he submerged himself in profound exchanges of divine knowledge and delved into the mystical art of healing through the touch of his hands—a spiritual practice now acknowledged as reiki.

Much like Buddha and Muhammad, Jesus ascended to enlightenment—an elevated state of superconsciousness achieved through personal exertion, dedicated learning, and unwavering commitment. At this pivotal juncture, he unraveled the mysteries of existence, the cycles of life and death, the roots of human suffering, and the profound power of healing.

This transformative phase marked Jesus' reemergence in Christian history, chronicled in the Bible. Thereafter, according to recorded history, he embarked on a soul-searching sojourn, retreating into the wilderness for forty days and forty nights, abstaining from food while seeking communion with the divine. Emerging from this celestial spiritual ordeal, he was imbued with the power of the spirit, launching into a mission of preaching, healing, and imparting the mystical truths he had discovered. Paralleling the experiences of Buddha and Muhammad, this moment encapsulates his enlightenment—a culmination of inner metamorphosis and divine revelation.

To grasp the divine essence of Jesus' teachings, one must delve into the simplicity of his messages. His proclamation to 'wake up' directly addressed the state of our unconscious mind, urging us to be aware and conscious of our thoughts, emotions, and desires. The commandment to 'love your neighbour as yourself' underscored the paramount significance of love as a unifying force, bridging the gap between the unconscious and conscious mind—authentic neighbors in the truest sense. When he declared, 'If you do not become like a child, you cannot enter the kingdom of heaven,' Jesus laid out a straightforward roadmap. It delineated a step-by-step approach to reclaim the joy, freedom, and playfulness of childhood—a transformative journey from unconsciousness to consciousness, culminating in the elevated state of superconsciousness, where one reunites with the divine essence—the soul or spirit within.

It is noteworthy that the teachings of Jesus, Buddha, Muhammad, and Guru Nanak exhibit striking similarities. While the language and styles may differ due to the epochs they lived in, the underlying purpose remains consistent—to liberate humanity from the confines of rigid traditions and religious divisions and guide individuals towards a deeper understanding of their unconscious feelings, desires, and motivations. Paradoxically, humanity has often moved in the opposite direction, sinking further into unconsciousness and exacerbating religious divisions. Instead of transcending traditions, more religious barriers have been erected in their names, posing a threat to the very unity of humankind. This paradox becomes even more evident when we shift our attention to the modern world, where divisions now manifest not only through religion but also through contrasting ways of life.

Let us now turn our attention to the contemporary world we inhabit—a realm broadly divided into two domains, East and West, reflecting a dichotomy much like that between consciousness and unconsciousness. In the West, denizens have ardently embraced a materialistic ethos, vigorously pursuing self-sufficiency, acquiring life's comforts, ensuring bread on the table complemented by a glass of wine. Through their assiduous endeavours, they have attained a commendable degree of prosperity.

Presently, a majority of Westerners enjoy a comfortable lifestyle, dwelling in resplendent homes, cruising in sophisticated automobiles, and adorning their abodes with the latest gadgets money can procure. However, in their relentless pursuit of materialism, they have inadvertently severed ties with the other facet of their being. They have neglected the profound verity that 'man cannot live by bread alone' and that flourishing in an unconscious world is an impossibility. Eventually, they awaken to the realisation that whatever material possessions they have amassed amount to nothing more than mere trinkets. In their quest for an enhanced life, they left a vital part behind, only to awaken one day to find themselves consciously bankrupt.

Consider the state of family life in the West. Close-knit familial bonds have become a rarity, and divorces are commonplace. Many individuals now opt to eschew marriage altogether, embracing convenient live-in relationships with fewer hassles and no commitments. Tragically, children from broken homes often grapple with finding their sense of identity and seek solace in drugs, alcohol, firearms, or promiscuity. Consequently, rehabilitation centres in the Western world are flourishing, witnessing a steady rise in the number of individuals seeking to overcome addiction. While the West has indeed achieved material abundance, becoming unconsciously affluent, it has concurrently grown impoverished in terms of consciousness.

In stark contrast, the denizens of the East have adhered to a less materialistic approach until recent times, remaining relatively unchanged. Their measured pursuit of specific goals has led to a dearth of remarkable success when compared to the West. For the majority of people in the East, the notion of a beautiful home or a nice car remains nothing more than a distant dream, and many still struggle to meet their daily basic needs. However, family life has mostly endured in this part of the world. Close-knit families are still prevalent, and divorces are not too common, as the institution of marriage holds immense significance in their lives.

Although the East may have retained its richness in conscious values, it has simultaneously remained unconsciously poor in terms of material abundance. Both regions find themselves ensnared in a state of discontent due to the profound imbalance that persists between consciousness and unconsciousness. It is essential to realise that one cannot be pursued at the expense of the other; rather, they are meant to coexist harmoniously. Just as we need both legs to move forward, attempting to proceed with just one will inevitably hinder our progress towards the desired destination. Similarly, can we fully appreciate the beauty of nature with only one eye? The joy derived would be incomplete, lacking wholeness.

The human race itself embodies the consequence of this gross imbalance between the conscious and unconscious mind. For centuries, we have been metaphorically deploying anger, ego, greed, and lust—the four prominent tools of unconsciousness—against one another. Countless wars have scarred history, continuing to rage, while terrorism inflicts untold destruction and suffering upon our world. Due to the extreme fluctuation in our internal energy levels, because of the improper balance between consciousness and unconsciousness, we have been figuratively blowing up, and in turn, annihilating the world around us. Our inner turmoil has become the architect of the destruction of our external universe. And the only way to attain true peace and serenity is through a balance, where consciousness and unconsciousness exist in equal measure.

Therefore, we must now embark on a profound journey to seek equilibrium within ourselves. We need to navigate the intricate labyrinth of our minds, in pursuit of that elusive middle point between the unconscious and conscious realms—a point where peace, stability, and illumination reside. This sacred middle path, discovered by Buddha upon his enlightenment, is the route he directed humankind to follow for the alleviation of suffering and liberation from pain. Put simply, our mission is to elevate our consciousness while simultaneously diminishing unconsciousness. Both aspects must co-exist in equal measure, maintaining a harmonious fifty-fifty balance, for their union to bestow upon us true harmony. And when conscious and unconscious finally merge, an entirely new reality unfurls before us—a realm abounding with unlimited possibilities. This is the domain of the un-manifested mystical world, the state of enlightenment, nirvana, salvation, liberation from the cycles of birth and death, and ultimately the state of superconsciousness.

Having embarked on this illuminating journey and attained an understanding of the conscious, unconscious, and superconscious states, we shall now delve into the ways and means of reaching this celestial destination. Although the path may be long and winding, with a dedicated approach, it is also adorned with profound moments of self-discovery, understanding, and awakening. This journey beckons us to nurture the seeds of love within, allowing them to grow into a forest of serenity that shelters not only our own souls but also those we encounter on this shared path of enlightenment.

Chapter 4
Understanding and Healing the Inner Child

Embracing the Wounded Healer Within

In the enchanting realm of our existence, the inner child—our unconscious mind—emerges as an undeniable reality. This wondrous entity, repository of our past experiences spanning countless lifetimes, stands as a testament to the profound evolution of our very being since the dawn of time. It also holds within it the courage and seemingly miraculous abilities to accomplish extraordinary feats. Such acts reveal the supernatural prowess of the inner child—an enigmatic force endowed with creativity, intuition, and an uncanny grasp of the tapestry of past, present, and future.

Moreover, within the inner child lie the deeply embedded shadows of our emotional vault—a storehouse of repressed emotions, past wounds, and feelings of isolation and sorrow. This realm houses the darker facets of our psyche, embracing the fires of anger, unfulfilled yearnings, primal instincts, and a latent unrest that slumbers within. Alas, the daunting fear of facing this shadowy realm coerces us to evade the embrace of its intrinsic negativity. Ironically, when we find ourselves disliking certain traits in others, we are unwittingly gazing upon reflections of our own concealed flaws—a mystic mirror that unveils our truth.

It is crucial to recognise that this inner child is the manifestation of our own creation and the gradual evolution of our physical and mental states. Over innumerable lifetimes, our insecurities and unresolved negativity have been unknowingly projected onto this vulnerable entity, inflicting profound pain and leading to the development of certain habits and emotional traits. In the relationship between the conscious mind, which acts as a parent, and the unconscious mind, which functions as the child, a delicate balance must be struck. This is vital because in any encounter, the child invariably emerges as the dominant and triumphant force.

To witness this profound phenomenon, one only needs to engage in a simple yet illuminating experiment. Picture a child who hesitates to undertake a particular task. Entice him with a promise of his heart's deepest desires and watch as he willingly embraces the challenge. Thus, a mutual accord unfolds—an equitable pact devoid of victors or losers.

Now, envision a scenario where the child seeks something from you. Deny it and see what happens. Without wasting any time, the child will begin crafting situations, employing a myriad of subtle persuasions to attain his desired goal. You may not even realise what is happening and end up giving him what you had earlier denied. The most intriguing part is that you will not even have the slightest clue that this was a well-planned game, in which the child emerged victorious while you unknowingly yielded to their enchanting wiles.

Why does this beguiling play unfold in this manner? Simply because the parent slumbers, oblivious to the subtle maneuvers of the child's games. And in a captivating parallel, our unconscious mind mirrors the child's maneuvers throughout the tapestry of our lives. Like an artful child, it orchestrates scenarios that aim to dominate and control, wielding extraordinary powers unbeknownst even to our conscious selves. In fact, the very essence of hypnosis—a mysterious and captivating art—lies in the profound communion with the unconscious mind, as the conscious self descends into a temporary slumber, granting passage to an extraordinary dialogue with the inner child.

So, when adults display intriguing eccentricities or grapple with elusive fears, the roots are often found in the realms of the unconscious, reaching back to the traumas that unfolded during those pivotal first seven cycles of growth. This is why the unconscious is often seen as a treasure trove of memories, holding the echoes of our past births—threads that a skilled hypnotist can access to unravel the mysteries of our previous lives. Thus, the magical dance of the inner child emerges as an awe-inspiring marvel that resides at the heart of our soul's extraordinary odyssey through the uncharted realms of existence.

Let me share a scenario that demonstrates the mystical grip of the unconscious mind upon our lives through a fascinating encounter I had with a retired couple living in the vibrant city of Los Angeles. Each week, during their routine trips to the local supermarket, they diligently filled their shopping cart with cherished items like green tea and coconut biscuits. And on one fateful day, I found myself accompanying them on this mundane errand, and as we unpacked the shopping bags upon returning home, I stood in awe of the sight before me—approximately twenty packs of both green tea and coconut biscuits meticulously arranged in their cupboard, enough to sustain them for a good half-year. And yet, despite this abundance, they proceeded to add two more packs of each item to their stockpile.

This seemingly perplexing behaviour intrigued me a lot and in the ensuing days, I embarked on a gentle quest to unravel the enigmatic behavioural pattern of this charming elderly couple. Ever mindful of their sentiments, I refrained from probing them directly, instead engaging them in heartfelt conversations that gently traced the steps of their past, back to their wondrous childhood days. As I delved into their memories, a remarkable revelation unfolded—the roots of their curious behaviour lay in a distant country where food shortages were a haunting reality, and essential items were a rarity, often unavailable for prolonged periods. Though now settled in Los Angeles, a city where such scarcities were unheard of, as the supply perpetually exceeded the demand, their unconscious minds clung to the echoes of the past. The shortages they endured during their tender years had imprinted indelibly upon their inner child. Now, as seasoned adults, that inner child, unknown to them, sought to compensate for those past deprivations, resulting in their ongoing compulsion to stockpile provisions as if preparing for an unseen scarcity.

In the grand tapestry of humanity, the poignant tale of this wonderful couple is but a reflection of a larger truth that echoes across countless lives where adults, in their crucial formative years, were deprived of the bountiful embrace of unconditional love and mindful care. In those initial seven years of growth, as the first body took shape, genuine love and mutual understanding between parents were a rarity, leaving indelible marks upon the tender souls of their innocent offspring. It is a yearning that reverberates in the hearts of many, a profound ache for the nurturing touch of a love that would have instilled in them an enduring sense of belonging and security.

So, just as a balanced budget ensures the stability of an economy, a harmonious and balanced marriage holds the key to producing and nurturing stable children. When two souls unite in matrimony, they create a sacred space wherein the seeds of love, compassion, and understanding can take root and flourish. In the previous chapter, I delved deeply into the very essence of marriage, emphasising its true meaning, which extends far beyond the realm of individual desires. It serves as the vital foundation for the well-being and flourishing of our future generations. The foundation upon which we build our house determines its strength and stability. We might construct a grand dwelling adorned with marble floors, golden chandeliers, and lavish furniture, but if the foundation is weak, a mere jolt or a minor earthquake could bring it crashing down like a house of cards. Similarly, the strength and nature of our inner child are shaped by the foundation laid by our parents during those formative years.

Psychiatrists have affirmed that during a child's initial years, specifically the first seven, their mind is remarkably receptive and telepathic. Not only do they absorb the sensory input of what they see and hear, but the thoughts and emotions of those in close proximity also leave a lasting impression on their unconscious mind. It is therefore crucial for parents to remain mindful of their own thoughts and emotions as their children grow and develop. With this awareness, they hold the power to profoundly shape their children's lives, guiding them to evolve into extraordinary individuals by embodying the very qualities they wish to see flourish in them.

Beyond Illusion: Discovering True Love

In the modern world, the essence of love has been gravely misconstrued. Today you may claim to love someone, and tomorrow that love may fade; today you fall in love, get married, and within a few years, you find yourself divorced.

We have reduced love to a fleeting emotion, a passing attraction, where we fall in love with a person one day and fall out of it the next. Such superficiality reveals that it was never true love to begin with. Sometimes, we may be attracted merely to the outward appearance of someone, failing to truly delve into their heart. This tendency is part of our normal human behaviour as what may seem beautiful and captivating today might lose its allure tomorrow, and in time, even turn unattractive. Strangely, we accept and rationalise such changes as an ordinary course of events.

What we must understand is that genuine love is not a fleeting affair, here today and gone tomorrow. Instead, it is an intrinsic part of our true selves. Even the scriptures reverberate with the proclamation: 'Love is God, and God is love.' Additionally, love is the nourishment for our souls, a celestial force that nurtures our inner child and propels us towards greater consciousness. The highest spiritual teaching lies in loving one another, but can one truly love another if love does not reside within? Can we feed a beggar when we have no food to offer? Moreover, how can we even dream of genuinely loving someone else when we haven't even learnt to love ourselves?

The scenario of numerous love marriages worldwide echoes a similar pattern: today, they are a picture of beauty and harmony, and tomorrow, they descend into discord and turmoil. With great pomp and show, couples tie the knot, often depleting their life savings or resorting to loans to create a grand wedding spectacle, all in an attempt to prove the authenticity of their love. Yet, in a relatively short period, the mounting legal fees and related stress reveal the impending collapse of their passionate love affair, as it now hurtles towards the courtroom.

This prevailing state of love marriages is commonplace in the Western world, but the East is rapidly catching up, determined not to lag behind in the pursuit of such superficial love. While the East is renowned for its continued practice of arranged marriages, the West struggles to comprehend how can one marry or be in love with someone they hardly know. It epitomises a difference in ideology—two distinct ways of life, one driven by materialism, the other by a quest for spirituality. Let's take a closer look at this duality.

Materialism holds dominion over the external aspects of life, catering to our physical needs, while spirituality delves into our inner reality—a profound search for love, ever-existent within the spirit itself. Arranged marriages find their origins in the belief that everything is preordained, with unions divinely destined in the heavens, celebrated through earthly life. In contrast, love marriages necessitate an intimate understanding of one another to fall in love. However, after the wedding vows are exchanged, many couples awaken to the harsh reality that they hardly know each other. During courtship, each lover showcases their conscious side—the finest version of themselves, always eager to please. Yet, post-marriage, the unconscious facets of our nature, shaped by childhood conditioning, begin to surface, revealing the less attractive traits we concealed during courtship. As this hidden side of the unconscious mind manifests, the grip of love gradually weakens, and the outward beauty that initially captivated easily succumbs to the ugliness within.

In arranged marriages, the dynamics are quite the opposite, with the concept of outer beauty playing a minimal role. Nowadays, prospective partners do meet and discuss their likes, hobbies, and dreams before entering matrimony. However, in the past, parents arranged the union, and the couple laid eyes on each other for the first time on their wedding night. Their journey of understanding and discovering one another commenced from there, with the primary aim of exploring their inner beauty, purity, and gradually falling in love with each other's inner selves. This served as the fundamental principle of arranged marriages, and back then, children had immense trust and love for their parents, wholeheartedly accepting the partner of their parents' choice. They entered this sacred alliance without even glimpsing the person with whom they were to spend their entire lives. Inner beauty held true significance, forming the essence of their lives.

Today, the profound trust and love that once bound parents and children together seem to have become elusive. Unbeknownst to them, parents have inadvertently left scars on their children during their formative years, fracturing the intimate bond with their innocent hearts. This disconnection has unfolded unconsciously, leaving us with a fragmented relationship with our own inner child—a part of us yearning to be heard and embraced. The inner child within each of us is crying out for healing; it craves extensive restoration, as the positive elements of our unconscious mind have been overshadowed by a plethora of fears, insecurities, dogmas, and misguided religious conditioning planted in our minds from an early age.

This fractured bond with the inner child often shapes how we seek love and validation in our lives. This is the reason why, in our pursuit of self-love and acceptance, it is common for us to focus on cherishing our outer selves. We invest considerable time, effort, and energy into cultivating our physical appearance—whether through grooming, fashion, or fitness—in a bid to present the most beautiful version of ourselves to the world. When we gaze into a mirror, we behold what we consider the loveliest person in the world. However, just as we lavish love on our external appearance, we must learn to extend the same affection to our inner selves. For far too long, we have been conditioned to place more importance on the outer shell, neglecting the profound beauty and power that reside within. It is time to recognise that, in the pursuit of wholeness, we must cultivate love and acceptance for the entirety of who we are—inside and out.

Awakening the Magic Within

As discussed earlier, one of the most overlooked and yet vitally important aspects of ourselves is the inner child—the pure, dormant potential that lies within all of us, waiting to be discovered and embraced. Often, due to past experiences, societal pressures, and emotional wounds, we bury this part of ourselves deep within the recesses of our unconscious mind. Over time, we lose touch with this vibrant source of creativity, imagination, and untapped talent. But once we begin the courageous journey of dismantling the barriers that have kept this part of us hidden away, we will be astonished by the abundance of natural talent that lies within. It is through this profound reconnection to our inner child that we can begin to unearth our supernatural energies, unlocking abilities and gifts we never realised we possessed. These talents are not born from external validation, but from the untainted purity of our innermost being. And when we reconnect with our inner child, we free ourselves from the constraints of self-doubt and fear. In doing so, we ignite our hearts and souls and inspire others to do the same, empowering them to achieve greatness.

When we wholeheartedly embrace and nurture our inner child with love, the result is the emergence of remarkable individuals who leave an indelible mark on the world. Successful artists, athletes, healers, inventors, and businesspeople draw upon the powers of their inner child, reaching new heights of creativity, intuition, and achievement. These individuals tap into the innate potential that resides within them, and their careers become a symphony of greatness—an expression of who they are at their core. Their accomplishments are extraordinary, their impact far-reaching, and their contributions to the world transformative. With their hearts and minds unified, they become beacons of inspiration, illuminating the path for others to follow. This, in essence, is the reality of our being and our true purpose on earth—to awaken and bring forth our natural talents, to use them in service to one another, and to create a world that celebrates the full spectrum of human potential.

In the captivating realms of the 1982 Hollywood classic *E.T. the Extra-Terrestrial* and its culturally resonant 2003 Bollywood adaptation *Koi Mil Gaya*, the profound bond of love and trust between an alien and a child unfolds with enchanting brilliance. These cinematic masterpieces transcend cultural barriers to reveal the innate power of compassion, love, and talent that reside in the hearts of children. In both films, we are entranced by the heartwarming portrayal of a child's protectiveness and care towards an otherworldly visitor, whose very existence holds the key to unlocking a higher potential. Witnessing the child's relentless efforts to reunite the alien with its real world ignites a spark of hope for the pure and selfless nature of the human spirit—a spirit that seeks connection, love, and understanding above all else. This bond between the child and the alien reflects the transformative power of the inner child within each of us, patiently waiting to be awakened and embraced.

In *Koi Mil Gaya*, the alien—affectionately named Jadu (meaning magic)—bestows upon the protagonist, Rohit, a gift that transforms his very essence. Though an adult, Rohit possesses within him the purity and innocence of a child, a quality that unlocks his latent potential when touched by Jadu. This interaction, gentle yet profound, catalyses a metamorphosis that sees Rohit blossom into a supernatural being, adept in academics, athletics, and the arts, becoming an exemplar of what it means to awaken the hidden potential that lies within all of us. His transformation is not merely a shift in physical ability but a rekindling of the innate brilliance that, much like a forgotten treasure, lies untouched within every soul. As Jadu gently places his glowing hand on Rohit's head, the inactive energy within him surges to life, unveiling extraordinary talents he never knew he had.

This transformation symbolises something much deeper, a universal truth that we are often blind to in our modern world: the power to achieve greatness lies within us all, locked away by the walls we build around our inner child. The adults in these films—those who fail to understand the alien's true nature—

are fixated on power, wealth, and control. Driven by selfish ambition, they seek to exploit the visitor from beyond for personal gain. Had they succeeded in their attempt to capture and dissect the alien, it would have met a tragic fate, stripped of its essence, much like how we, too, strip away the magic of our inner child by allowing societal pressures and misguided conditioning to rule our lives. Instead of nurturing this profound part of ourselves, we subject it to the harsh realities of a world that often values conformity over individuality, stifling the very qualities that make us unique and powerful.

Such tales weave a metaphor that transcends the silver screen and finds resonance in our own lives. Just as the alien embodies the magic of the unknown and the unexpressed, so too does our inner child hold the key to unlocking untapped talents and boundless potential. When these powers remain dormant, they are overlooked and disregarded—until an alien, pure in heart and unburdened by the weight of the world, sees beyond the surface and reawakens the magical potential buried deep within the protagonist. In much the same way, we are all born with innate gifts, yet these treasures are often buried under the weight of societal expectations and fears. The child within each of us waits patiently, yearning to be rediscovered, ready to reignite the flame of greatness that quietly flickers inside.

Yet, while stories reveal the wonder of hidden gifts, reality often presents us with systems that fail to nurture them. In today's educational systems, this inner potential remains largely unexplored, overshadowed by a focus on conventional metrics of success—grades, wealth, and social standing. These systems, built on rigid structures of conformity and standardisation, impose a one-size-fits-all approach to learning, neglecting the individual spark of creativity and originality that makes each child unique. Instead of encouraging the discovery of our true gifts, these systems prioritise uniformity, stifling the innate brilliance that every child possesses. It is as if we are pressing our children into molds that ignore the rich diversity of their souls, preventing them from flourishing into the individuals they are meant to become.

The Pareto Principle, the 80-20 rule, echoes this inequality. It reveals that only a small percentage of people are able to tap into their true potential, while the vast majority remain trapped in cycles of limitation and unfulfilled promise. This principle is not confined to wealth; it speaks to a larger, deeper truth about the imbalance of opportunity, creativity, and success in our society. Only a few are given the resources and space to nurture their talents, while the rest of us are left to grapple with a system that often fails to recognise our individuality and the gifts we hold. The education system, by failing to acknowledge the distinct abilities and potential of each child, perpetuates this inequality, leaving many to live lives unfulfilled, unable to access the greatness within them.

The time has come for this to change. It is no longer enough to revise curricula or impose superficial reforms. What is needed is a shift in the very philosophy of education itself—an approach that recognises and nurtures the whole child, i.e., mind, body, and spirit. Just as the alien in *Koi Mil Gaya* reveals the vast world of potential hidden beneath the surface, we, too, must provide children with the right environment and tools to awaken the latent magic within them. Education should not be a passive process of information absorption; it should be an active, transformative journey that encourages self-discovery, emotional growth, and the cultivation of unique abilities.

If we embrace this model of education, we can break the cycle of inequality that the 80-20 rule illuminates. By fostering environments where children are encouraged to explore their individual talents—whether in the arts, sciences, sports, or social change—we can make self-realisation accessible to all. We can make success not a privilege for the few, but a universal possibility for all. Through education that celebrates creativity, self-awareness, and personal growth, we can unlock the immense, untapped potential within every child. And in doing so, we will create a world where innovation, compassion, and creativity flourish, where every individual has the opportunity to rise to their fullest self, just as Rohit, the protagonist, rises to meet his extraordinary potential when he reconnects with the magic of his inner child.

Thus, we must reimagine education on a global scale—one that unlocks the true power of the unconscious mind and ensures that children are not subjected to the corrosive influence of toxic ideologies or manipulative teachings. Through an education that nurtures creativity, critical thinking, and self-awareness, we equip future generations with the tools to discover and refine their innate abilities, empowering them to contribute positively to society and to build a world founded on peace, love, and understanding. Only by transforming education to focus on the holistic development of every child can we unleash the boundless power of human potential.

Beyond Quick Fixes: The Path of True Healing

When it comes to healing, it is vital to examine our approach—do we simply mask the discomfort, or do we bravely seek its root? True healing begins with understanding the underlying cause, much like a doctor who must first diagnose the illness before prescribing treatment. On this journey of self-healing, we must step into the role of our own physician, choosing our remedies with care. The challenge lies in resisting the temptation of quick fixes, which, like much of modern medicine, often ease the symptoms but fail to address the deeper cause. Let's explore this aspect in greater detail.

Modern medicines, while providing temporary relief, do not truly cure ailments and often come with harmful side effects that hinder the body's self-healing process. They wield a double-edged sword, demanding patients to recover not once, but twice—first from the illness and then from the effects of the prescription. The fact is that the root cause of any disease lies in the free flow of toxins within our bodies, created by emotional disturbances, unhealthy food, lack of physical exercise, and other factors. Unfortunately, modern medicines may exacerbate this toxicity when the body is least capable of coping with it. Therefore, the true power to cure lies not in these medicines, but in the embrace of nature.

As the esteemed Hippocrates, the father of medicine, wisely proclaimed, it is nature itself that cures and not the physician. This profound wisdom is equally applicable to us in our quest to heal our inner child; the right prescription lies in reconnecting with nature. Our true nature is consciousness, and through heightened self-awareness, we can gain the ability to accurately diagnose our inner struggles. At the root of our problems lies the accumulation of toxins within our unconscious mind, formed by deep-rooted belief systems, traditions, ego, and erroneous ideologies. The antidote to cleanse this state of acute toxicity is love, the very essence that the inner child lacked during its crucial formative years. Put simply, the solitary obstruction hindering our growth is our inner child, fervently yearning for restoration through the tender embrace of unconditional love.

To conclude, it is important to remember that each individual carries the responsibility for their unique journey of growth and evolution. There exists no age threshold to this advancement; the only barrier that hinders our progress is internal, and it is solely through inner exploration that genuine learning unfolds. For far too long, we have embarked on an outward expedition, deeply enmeshed in the material world and the ceaseless pursuit of dominion. The time has arrived to initiate an inner quest and mend the child within. We may have sought the mysteries of creation in the external scientific domain, yet the mystical wisdom lies nestled within our inner sanctuaries. Our sole task is to initiate and unfurl our boundless possibilities. Countless spiritual teachings underscore the simple veracity that everything resides within us, and what stands before and behind us pales in significance compared to the vastness within. And as we delve deeper into our inner self, the purpose behind our existence and the authentic essence of life will gradually unfold.

Chapter 5

Ego as the Primary Barrier to Growth

The Silent Architect of Division

Unseen yet ever-present, ego drifts through the corridors of the mind like an invisible current. It does not reveal itself openly but hides within subtle impulses—an unspoken need to be right, a restless craving for recognition, a quiet resistance to surrender. You will not find it in bold declarations but in the unease it leaves behind in the form of a disruption of harmony, a loss of simplicity, and a fracture in peace.

Ego, in its many forms, stands as the most formidable barrier between the human soul and the realm of enlightenment. It is the silent architect of division, the unseen force that breeds arrogance, and the greatest thief of wisdom. It constructs walls between self and other, between man and divinity, between wisdom and ignorance. It blinds us to the interconnectedness of existence, convincing us that our intellect alone is the source of knowledge.

Additionally, ego tempts us to believe that power is ours to wield, that we stand as sovereigns over life's unfolding script. Yet, history serves as a testament to the frailty of this illusion. Kings, conquerors, and rulers have risen and fallen, believing themselves invincible—only to be humbled by time's unyielding hand. The ego-driven pursuit of dominance has left empires in ruins and hearts in turmoil.

The ego's power lies in enshrouding us in a cocoon of self-centred thoughts, elevating our own interests above all else. It coerces us into an unrelenting pursuit of validation for our correctness, birthing a fabricated aura of superiority, and presents itself as an indomitable barrier to our healing and spiritual evolution. The seeds of ego take root in tandem with the development of our unconscious mind, their tendrils unfurling during the inaugural seven-year cycle of existence. While the growth of unconscious tapers off by age seven, the ego does not languish; it continues to grow and expand endlessly throughout the entire course of our earthly journey, each year bolstering its monstrous dominion.

The origins of this egoic ascent are primarily woven into the fabric of religious belief systems, intricately crafted by the hands of parents and predecessors. Right from the inception of birth, a child is bestowed with the brand of Hindu, Sikh, Buddhist, Christian, or Muslim, deeply embedding the stamp of ego identification within the sanctified realms of the unconscious mind. During this nascent phase of growth, the child stands as a pristine canvas, pure and untainted by the complexities of the material world. Untouched by the divisive lines of sectarianism, ethnicity, race, colour, or creed that lie ahead, they bask in the innocence of their celestial existence.

Throughout history, various religions have sought to assert their dominion over others. Devotees have invested endless years in the endeavour to substantiate their faith's founders as the chosen emissaries of the divine, tasked with illuminating the world with the radiance of consciousness. Fueling this quest for supremacy, they staunchly uphold the belief that awakening, nirvana, salvation, or liberation can only be achieved through unwavering adherence to the guidelines laid down within their respective sacred scriptures.

The pursuit of superiority over others—the very essence of ego-identification—has been the catalyst for spreading world religions, resulting in the sectarian division that pervades our manifested world. Countless wars have been waged and continue to ravage our planet, perpetuating hatred and fear and leading to ruthless mass murders of innocent people and the wanton destruction of religious and historical monuments, all in the name of religion and ethnicity. History bears witness to this persistent treachery that divides the world today.

The key point to note here is that what unfolds on the stage of history is but a reflection of the hidden struggles that originate within the depths of the human psyche. Deep within the labyrinth of the unconscious mind, the ego arises as a complex force, endlessly driven by an intense fear of its own demise. This primal dread assumes a pivotal role in the ego's development, driving it to construct a formidable fortress of defensive mechanisms in a desperate bid to survive. The deep-rooted anxiety woven into the very fabric of the ego's foundation becomes unmistakably evident in its unyielding compulsion to assert dominance during arguments.

Inevitably, the inner tension of the ego seeks an outlet, and it finds its battleground in the clash of voices and wills. This is evident in situations where, caught in the heat of debate, neither participant is willing to yield, for to do so feels to the ego like annihilation. In the arena of marital discord, the stakes may escalate dramatically, potentially leading to the eruption of a physically violent altercation. Tragically, in such dire instances, the ego's stronghold of superiority often manifests in the form of a man raising his hand against his female partner. This behaviour stems from deeply ingrained societal conditioning, where men have historically occupied positions of power and dominance, leaving a deep impression on the collective psyche that inadvertently perpetuates inequality. Even in this contemporary age, the most formidable nation on the global stage, the USA, remains bereft of a woman leader, a poignant testament to the unrelenting dominion of ego in a society that occasionally elevates men, who continue to denigrate women in the most egregious manner.

Such is the character of ego—long shrouded in a spectral veil, a phantom-like nature that casts shadows upon our perceptions. Even within the expanse of the divine realm, the concept of God predominantly assumes a male form, always invoking the resolute pronoun 'He,' never the nurturing 'She,' embodying the all-encompassing role of a father rather than the gentle grace of a mother. Yet can we truly confine our ineffable essence, our authentic being, our soul or spirit within the narrow precincts of gender? How, then, can we ascribe such limitations to the infinite concept of God?

Moreover, the ego, driven by the relentless fear of death, continues to spawn situations and ideologies. The loss of an argument equates to a symbolic demise; the inability to establish superiority over another is a reality the ego refuses to embrace. Each fractured relationship, shattered marriage, or eroded friendship becomes a testimony to the ego's unyielding aversion to death. The dissolution of these bonds remains inconsequential as the survival of the ego emerges as the paramount concern. The demise of ego, under any circumstances, is a proposition not to be entertained.

Our ego has etched an indelible mark in shaping the course of the world we inhabit. The schisms that pervade our existence will only deepen until we grapple with the monstrous nature of the ego. The fact is that the egoic tendencies of humanity persist, perpetuating the chasm and hatred all throughout the world. It is the ego-identification of humanity that has skewed its perception of reality. Thus, it becomes crucial to bring these elementary truths into the clear light of consciousness, for only then is the true essence of the ego revealed.

The Many Faces of Ego

While the ego is essentially formless, it assumes myriad manifestations. The primary ones encompass religious affiliation, societal standing, wealth and acquisitions, physical appearance, racial heritage, national identity, political allegiance, sports affiliation, and an unwavering compulsion to be right in every circumstance.

As mentioned earlier, the seeds of egoistic patterns germinate early, manifesting discernibly after the first seven-year cycle of growth. As the child matures, the urge to appear finer, draped in more resplendent attire than their companions, takes root. They may yearn for their parents to possess the grandest abode or the finest automobile in the vicinity, nurturing a false sense of pride and an illusory air of ascendancy. Ironically, in their early years, while engaged with toys, such ego remains nonexistent. During this phase, if they encounter a toy at a friend's residence that they lack, their request is straightforward—to obtain the same toy, not a superior one. When the child, in such instances, cries or fusses over what they have just glimpsed, a common parental response echoes, 'Stop crying and behave yourself. Tomorrow

I shall acquire an even finer one for you.' Though the child may persist that their desire is not for a superior version but for the identical item, the seed of ego—a yearning for the better—is unknowingly sown within their unconscious mind.

In countless ways, both consciously and unconsciously, parents plant these seeds in their children during their formative years. Their ego-driven insistence that the child must excel in academics, sports, or other pursuits profoundly shapes the child's ego development. Instead of nurturing the virtues of sincere effort, dedication, and diligence to achieve goals, parents often end up teaching their children how to simply rise above their peers. Eventually, this conditioning gradually exacts its toll on the tender soul of the child.

This also gives rise to a fear that constantly whispers the dread of falling short of the towering expectations set by parents. In a paradoxical twist, a profound reality emerges—striving to satisfy a parent's desires is like chasing a horizon that forever recedes from the child's grasp. Today's triumphs and the heights achieved in various pursuits soon turn into tomorrow's demand for more. And when this endless yearning goes unfulfilled, discontent becomes a constant companion in their lives.

Additionally, the ego, camouflaging weakness as strength, bears the brunt of failure in meeting coveted expectations. This becomes evident in moments of failure, when the ego, like an earthquake, shakes the inner realm with a force that shatters all equilibrium. From this fracture arises a deeper turbulence, one that drives the ego into even greater frenzy. The repercussions of failure, as harbingers of impending doom, pale in significance as the ego's obsession with achievement gains momentum. The axiom 'survival of the fittest' now finds itself replaced with an updated maxim, 'survival of the egoist,' a testament to the ethos of today's world. In this ego-driven realm, survival mandates the bending and breaking of rules that once underpinned human conduct. Sacred vows and commitments have lost their sanctity; the hallowed principles that guided humanity have been supplanted by a ruthless arena, a battleground where ethical anchors have eroded, leaving the landscape barren of morals and devoid of ethics in the realms of business, society, politics, and interpersonal relationships.

Within this landscape, parents find themselves incomplete when their offspring falter, while children grapple with a sense of insufficiency, failing to match the towering standards set for them. Roots of unworthiness intertwine themselves into their very core, compelling them to seek solace elsewhere. When adolescents veer off course, gravitating towards drugs, violence, and precocious liaisons, it is the gnawing sense of inadequacy that propels them down these perilous paths. Clinical observers of human behaviour, psychiatrists, affirm that individuals who engage in such conduct often harbour feelings of insufficiency and unworthiness.

The simple truth here is that at the very core of our being, we humans yearn for completeness, for affection and acknowledgement. When this yearning remains unfulfilled, we embark on a relentless quest for affluence, material possessions, social acclaim, or flutter from one relationship to another, caught in an endless chase for ascendancy and enrichment. With every triumph, the ego finds fleeting gratification as its appetite for satisfaction is insatiable—a concept that remains alien to its very existence. Thus, it keeps ascending, unbounded by peaks, as the sense of satiation eludes its grasp. For instance, today you might set your sights on amassing a million dollars, convinced it holds the key to your happiness and contentment. Yet, as that milestone draws near, the ego, insatiable as ever, will already be gesturing towards the next million, and the chase will persist indefinitely. Due to this reason, the colossal phantom, the ego, continues to stand triumphantly, having cast its sprawling shadow across the entirety of human existence.

Breaking Free from the Cage of Ego

The ego possesses an innate propensity for expansion as it remains perpetually dissatisfied with any fixed position and never accepts defeat, as that is akin to facing oblivion. Why does a civil discourse often devolve into a heated argument? The answer lies within the ego's refusal to accept defeat. In the throes of such encounters, relationships fracture, marriages splinter, and animosity brews, leaving us at odds with one another. The annals of history bear witness to countless divorce cases that have graced our courts and wars that have scarred our sacred earth—a bitter fruit of our egoic inclinations.

Comprehending the authentic nature of the ego emerges as the pivotal path to our metamorphosis and advancement. The route to this transformation lies in the nurturing of our true essence. This voyage into the self is akin to healing an ailment, where true resolution emerges only when the root cause is unearthed.

By now, you may have realised that these foundational roots rest in our religious beliefs and dogmas, steeped in tradition, and the insidious quest for supremacy over one another, both of which nourish the burgeoning ego. Thus, the antidote entails recognising these harmful components and methodically dismantling them, for they house the origin of humankind's most formidable adversary—the ego.

To relinquish the ego and shed the chains of tradition while our life force still courses through our veins requires undergoing a spiritual rebirth unencumbered by the weights of pessimistic and antiquated convictions. To postpone this awakening until the final embrace of physical death renders our endeavour inconsequential. The clarion call is to confront this reality now, liberating ourselves from the constricting clutches of time-honoured dogmas and emerging as rejuvenated beings, unburdened by the fetters of ancestral beliefs.

Throughout the annals of history, a cadre of spiritual masters and messengers dared to rise against the dominion of religious doctrines and the unconscious grip of egoic patterns entrenched in established world faiths and sects, often paying dearly for their audacity. Reflect upon Jesus, a towering figure crucified for defying the norms of conventional society and fearlessly striving to elevate the consciousness of those trapped in a state of unconsciousness. Modern religious leaders frequently proffer the notion that he died to absolve our sins. Yet, one may ponder: what transgressions do they refer to? Can any sin exceed the grave error of persisting in an unconscious state, forsaking the trajectory of growth and evolution, wandering aimlessly like bewildered creatures in a jungle of illusions, ensnared by the dogmatic tenets of their sect?

In an intriguing experiment, a group of monkeys took centre stage. Five of them found themselves confined within a cage, while a solitary banana swayed tantalisingly in their midst. The very moment one of them mustered the courage to rise for the coveted fruit, the other four were met with a chilling spray of icy cold water. Following this, when a second monkey attempted the same feat, the remaining quartet once again found themselves drenched in the frigid cascade.

The narrative continued to unfold as a third monkey ascended in a determined pursuit of the banana. In response, the other four stood as an unyielding blockade, resolute in their effort to thwart its advance. At this juncture, one of the original quintet was discreetly withdrawn and replaced by a newcomer. This uninitiated participant leaped eagerly towards the banana upon sighting it, only to be met with the defiant resistance of its companions. Despite relentless attempts, the outcome remained unchanged, ultimately forcing the newcomer to resign in acquiescence.

As the experiment progressed, the scene repeated itself. Another monkey was exchanged with a new counterpart, and the pattern remained consistent—each attempt to acquire the banana was met with opposition from the other four. In subsequent phases, the remaining third, fourth and fifth members from the original group were sequentially replaced. With each new entrant, the same saga unfolded: a leap towards the banana and the resolute intervention of its companions. Curiously, the newcomers remained oblivious to the reason behind their thwarted endeavours. Furthermore, once the original five monkeys had been replaced, none of the substituted ones had experienced the sensation of the icy cold water spray. Yet, despite this, not a single monkey dared to rise and reach for the banana again.

What insight does this experiment bestow upon us? Why did the new monkeys abstain from pursuing their cherished fruit? The answer is uncomplicated: this behavioural pattern, established initially, had been embraced by all within the cage, leading any banana-centric endeavour to be met with collective resistance. In a parallel fashion, we often tread the path of religion, customs, and tradition without ever pausing to reflect upon our true essence, i.e., we are not mere animals; we are humans, endowed with intellect and free will. Should we not, then, exercise our freedom of thought, speech, and expression without hesitation, unburdened by fear? Alternatively, should we willingly confine ourselves within the cage of ill-conceived restrictions that limit our liberty?

For countless millennia, the ego has loomed as a formidable obstruction to the unfettered expression of our thoughts and freedom. Constantly entrenched in perpetual fear, the dread of demise becomes its wellspring of strength and restraining force. It finds solace and security by exerting control over human beings, much akin to the monkeys confined within the cage. When one summons the audacity to rise and break free from the constraints of societal norms, the ego swiftly responds defensively, endeavouring to draw them back into the confines of its traditional dominion.

To conclude this chapter, I would like to share a poetic symphony to encapsulate the quintessence of our existence ensnared within the cage of the ego.

Ego

An illusion nestled within the depths of the unconscious mind,
A stumbling stone,
Upon humanity's path to transcendence and enlightenment,
As pre-conceived notions entwine their grasp,
Believing our existence springs forth and continues,
Solely from the domains of our own inception.

Ego
A sensation of perpetual righteousness,
Visualising oneself as the saviour, the noble knight.
Harbouring an unswerving conviction,
That the knowledge and dominion one wields,
Dwells beyond the realms of judgement's reach.

Ego
A shadowy day and even darker night,
The paramount impediment,
To the advancement of the human tribe.

Ego
A negative bond between the conscious and unconscious mind,
Incapable of embracing divergent perspectives,
It obstructs inner reflections and dims the luminous vision.

Ego
The stark antithesis of our authentic nature,
History remains a steadfast witness,
To the heinous deeds of ego-driven individuals,
Who reckoned themselves above all,
In their pursuit of grandeur.

Ego
An illusion nestled within the depths of the unconscious mind,
A stumbling stone,
Upon humanity's path to transcendence and enlightenment.

The profound weight of these verses reveals the hidden chains that bind us, while also offering the key to overcoming the ego: the wisdom that we are never complete. Growth demands the humility to acknowledge our limitations, the openness to unlearn, and the courage to step beyond the self-imposed boundaries of certainty. Those who are truly enlightened do not cling to their opinions as absolute truths. Instead, they remain fluid, willing to evolve, willing to be wrong, willing to listen. The many sages, mystics, and enlightened beings who have walked before us all echo the same teaching: liberation begins where ego ends. Thus, the path to transcendence is not found in asserting one's superiority but in dissolving the illusion of self-importance.

Chapter 6

How Meditation Helps

From Darkness to Light

MEDITATION IS A STATE OF PROFOUND PEACE, A SANCTUARY for the mind to retreat from its ceaseless chatter. Our minds, like tireless machines, relentlessly produce thoughts, even in slumber when they manifest as dreams. Over time, this constant mental activity has rendered humanity powerless, allowing the mind to usurp the throne of our inner world, transforming the master into a servant.

The term 'meditation' often appears in dictionaries as deep contemplation. However, words, no matter how eloquent, can merely provide a glimpse of its true essence. You can describe light to someone who has lived their entire life in darkness, but as mere words, they remain hollow and insignificant, until that person experiences, feels, and witnesses light firsthand.

To understand this better, let us turn to an allegory from the ancient texts—a tale of an egocentric king who believed he would never die and that his rule would endure forever. With a harem of fifty wives and a legion of a hundred children, it was his firstborn son who became a source of grave anxiety. The king lived in constant dread that, just as he had wrestled the throne from his own father, his son would one day seek to dethrone him. Despite his unshakable confidence in his immortality and eternal rule, the ego, closely tied to the fear of death, took hold of him, and to quell this looming fear, he devised a plan.

The monarch constructed an underground palace, a subterranean realm where natural light and external influences were rigorously excluded. The queens were given stringent instructions never to divulge the existence of the world beyond to their children. A further measure was to prohibit any servant from entering this clandestine abode. This dual strategy aimed firstly to mitigate the risk of anyone inadvertently revealing details of the external world to the children and secondly, to keep the queens perpetually occupied with the grind of daily chores, leaving them with scant time for reflection upon the king's seemingly harsh actions, which deprived their offspring of the wonders of life.

The sole individual granted entry to the underground palace was the king himself. Every evening at four, he traversed a tunnel with his cart laden with fruits, vegetables, and other daily necessities to ensure a life of comfort for all within. Locks secured both the entrance and exit, with only he possessing the keys. After unlocking the front gate, he would enter with the cart, relocking it behind him, before joining his eagerly awaiting family. The first three hours upon his return were dedicated to imparting basic education and martial skills to his children. Despite the constraints imposed on their fundamental freedom, as a father, he did not shirk these essential responsibilities. Following these parental duties, he would spend the evening hours wining, dining, and sharing romantic moments with his queens. Then in the morning, he would depart at eight to attend to the affairs of his kingdom and return at four to his subterranean realm.

This routine persisted for many years as the children matured into adulthood. The eldest son reached the age of twenty-five, the traditional age for marriage in the kingdom. As a dutiful father, the king could not evade this responsibility, despite the deep conflict within him. The challenge of finding a bride who had lived in perpetual darkness, utterly ignorant of the external world and the distinctions between day and night, loomed insurmountable. Even if he kept her within the underground palace after the wedding, restraining her from revealing the world beyond with its nuances of darkness and light, to his son and others appeared implausible.

To resolve this quandary, the king devised a shrewd plan that served a dual purpose. He encountered a distant king who had only one cherished offspring, a beloved daughter. The mere thought of her departing after marriage filled him with dread. As the princess came of age at twenty, the king urgently sought a prince who would wed her and become an integral part of their kingdom. The two monarchs negotiated a matrimonial alliance, and the eldest son was dispatched to this far-off land.

For the first time in his life, as he departed his father's kingdom, the prince experienced the splendors of the outside world. Fresh air, blooming flowers, flowing rivers, serene ponds, and sparkling lakes greeted him. The first rays of sunlight infused new life into his being, instantly dispelling the twenty-five years of darkness. After two blissful years in this enchanting land, he ascended the throne following his father-in-law's demise. Since emerging from darkness into light, he had pondered the harsh realities of life, the fifty mothers and ninety-nine siblings he had left behind. By now, he had gained profound insight into why his father had kept them away from the world beyond, shielding them from the beauty and wonders of planet earth. Although he had gained freedom, his heart ached for his mothers, brothers, and sisters.

Upon assuming control of his new kingdom, he mustered his forces and spearheaded a rebellion against his father, culminating in the latter's defeat and ultimate demise. The prisoners of the underground palace were at long last emancipated; the shackles of darkness shattered by the radiance of light, and unconsciousness lifted from its shallow depths by the fragrance of an awakened conscious mind.

The analogy of this tale mirrors the purpose of meditation. It serves as a rebellion of consciousness against unconsciousness, which has imprisoned the entire human race within its subterranean palace, far away from the illuminating light, dwelling in perpetual darkness. It signifies a war against the unconscious forces of ego, hatred, anger, and greed—a transformative odyssey that guides humankind from darkness into the realm of forgiveness, beauty, wonders, love, and peace.

Beyond Methods, Toward Awareness

Now let's revisit the essence of meditation. Although the definition is inherently straightforward, the term meditation has grown complex over time, burdened by a plethora of books on the subject, and with an ever-expanding brigade of gurus and teachers who propagate various methods and techniques for attaining liberation, nirvana, awakening, or freedom. Therefore, let's meticulously dissect these words to comprehend what it truly means to engage in profound contemplation of spiritual matters. But a question that arises here is that can one truly focus on a matter of the spirit when surrounded by a crowd or even a few individuals? To delve deeply into one's thought processes, a requisite concentration is necessary, and solitude is paramount, free from any potential disruptions, not even the hum of a television, the chatter of a radio, or the distraction of a cell phone. The next question to consider is what precisely constitutes a spiritual matter? In simple terms, it relates to something inherently connected to the spirit, to one's soul. Moreover, to be spiritual does not necessitate regular visits to a temple, mosque, or church, for even in these holy places, one may find themselves immersed in a congregation—the very throng they should be seeking to escape. True closeness to one's spirit or soul can only be achieved in solitude.

Scriptures explicitly emphasise this, stating: 'And when you pray, you shall not be as the hypocrites are; for they love to pray standing in the temples and in the corners of the streets, that they may be seen by men. They will have their reward, but you, when you pray, enter your closet, and when you have shut the door, pray to the Father in secret; and your Father shall reward you openly.' The scriptures also endorse the proper manner of prayer, which closely resembles meditation. Visiting religious establishments to pray is merely a method to make one religious, and by adhering to such methods, one becomes religious in a systematic manner, akin to a robot programmed to conduct itself in a specific way. In this way, prayer turns into a mere tradition—a hindrance that keeps us from reaching our ultimate destination.

Meditation, though surrounded by countless methods, is often reduced to a crutch rather than a genuine path to deeper contemplation. A mantra, for instance, is meant to be a simple tool for setting intention. Yet when repeated mechanically, it risks becoming just another method that lulls the mind into a kind of sleep rather than awakening it. In such cases, the practice may offer temporary relief, much like ordinary rest, but it does little to stir true awareness. Therefore, mantras, postures, or other techniques can certainly provide structure, but they are not meditation itself. At best, they serve as entry points. The essence of meditation lies beyond method as it is the living process of awakening consciousness, of reconnecting with the spirit. That alone is its authentic purpose.

The meditative posture employed by Buddha, known as the lotus position, was not a method but rather a state in which he found comfort for meditation. However, his followers later turned this posture into a method and a tradition that every Buddhist is expected to follow. One must ponder how many of these followers have attained the meditative state, the pinnacle of enlightenment and nirvana that Buddha himself achieved. History awaits another Buddha, and this wait may be interminable unless we collectively grasp this reality and revise our perceptions of religion, tradition, and meditation.

The key takeaway here is that genuine meditation, much like authentic religion, transcends methods, techniques, mantras, and postures. It constitutes a process of inner growth and gradual evolution, a journey towards discovering our true nature. It embodies a comprehensive transformation, an overall enhancement of the human being, and a sacred transition from an unconscious state to one of consciousness. While methods can be useful tools to initiate the meditative process and cultivate the essential discipline for quiet introspection, they are not the sole essence of the practice.

Consider, for instance, the establishment of a business. Here, predetermined methods, rules, and regulations come into play. You must secure capital, register with the appropriate authorities, hire personnel, acquire, or construct facilities, and more. However, as operations commence, these methods gradually become redundant. To foster the growth and expansion of the company, intellect and innovative ideas are the driving forces. Examining the most prosperous individuals globally reveals that the empires they construct predominantly owe their success to novel and inventive concepts. Conversely, a significant number of businesspeople who adhere rigidly to methodical approaches often remain stagnant, barely sustaining their enterprises. Reflect on where Bill Gates might be today if he had adhered steadfastly to a fixed method in managing his business. Similarly, methods can indeed facilitate the initiation of the meditation process and nurture the discipline needed to carve out time for serene contemplation. Various methods are available, providing you with the flexibility to choose one according to your comfort level. Let me elucidate one of the simplest and most accessible methods.

Begin by meticulously selecting a quiet corner within your home, ensuring it serves as a sanctuary free from disturbances for at least twenty minutes. Sit either in a cross-legged position on the floor with a straight spine or in a chair with an upright backrest. Close your eyes and initiate the process with seven deliberate deep breaths. Consciously feel each inhalation as if originating from your abdomen, ascending through your chest, and exiting through your nostrils.

After this initial phase, return to normal breathing while exclusively focusing on the sensation of this motion. This involves concentrating on how the breath flows through your body, feeling the rise and fall of your chest and abdomen, and sensing the air passing through your nostrils.

In the initial stages, distractions may arise as your mind endeavours to divert your attention to diverse scenarios. Do not be concerned when this happens. The instant you discern your thoughts veering astray, gently steer your concentration back to your breathing. Sustain a consistent smile throughout this entire undertaking, as it significantly enhances your ability to focus.

This method serves as an optimal entry point, aimed at instilling inner discipline into your life. A method, akin to a computer software, acts as a facilitator. For instance, consider the software MS Word, which aids in composing a letter but cannot craft the message itself. It merely serves as a conduit. Similarly, this method functions as your MS Word—a gateway to your heart and soul. However, it is you who must carve out those twenty minutes to meditate in a tranquil corner. You are the author penning this letter, the voyager embarking on a journey into your inner realm, and ultimately the seeker who reaches the destination. Through consistent practice, you will evolve into a skilled writer and a seasoned traveler. When you reach a state where the mind is firmly anchored, free from its usual wanderings, the time comes to set aside this method and move to the next phase—the most crucial aspect of meditation: exploring the gap between consciousness and unconsciousness within the mind. The true essence of meditation lies in dedicating twenty minutes each day to this inner exploration.

This chasm between consciousness and unconsciousness maintains a ratio of ten to one. Put simply, this implies that after every ten unconscious thoughts, a single conscious thought enters the realm of our awareness. So, embarking on this journey unveils a staggering and at times, startling disparity between conscious and unconscious thoughts. Following the negative thoughts entwined with the roots of ego and its diverse branches of anger, hatred, jealousy, greed, and unyielding dominance, a lone positive thought acknowledging the preceding negativity emerges. It also becomes apparent that each negative thought brings forth repressed emotions such as fear and guilt, resulting in stress and discomfort, while the positive counterpart fosters confidence and the realisation that redemption is never too late. It provides an opportunity to mend relationships, rectify wrongs, and purge the body of the negativity sown by unconscious thoughts.

Once meditation helps you unearth these imperfections in your internal thought-process, your role transforms into that of a self-appointed mechanic tasked with repairing your own inner vehicle. The body or consciousness remains unscathed; it is solely the engine—your mind—that is faulty and requires a comprehensive overhaul. This extensive refurbishment is imperative to halt the production of excess negativity responsible for such thoughts, ultimately detrimental to our cells and organs, giving rise to an array of health issues.

The root cause of ninety per cent of the diseases afflicting human beings is this surplus negativity. Why do most individuals perpetually worry about the future, experiencing anxiety, nervousness, tension, and discontentment with their present life situation? Our body contains over thirty-seven trillion cells, each functioning as a tiny engine part of our inner world. These cells operate based on our thoughts, emotions, and expressions. The moment you become tense or anxious, signals are transmitted to them. A mere suggestion is all these cells require, and by fostering anxiety or stress, you are essentially generating negativity and inviting disease.

Thus, we can conclude that the actual cause of disease is nothing but anxiety and stress. And this is why meditation becomes indispensable, not just as a spiritual practice but as a vital tool to navigate life. It nurtures mental clarity, emotional balance, and physical well-being, offering harmony to both body and spirit.

Forgiveness: The Final Cure

Health is one of the deepest desires shared by all living beings, yet it remains one of humanity's greatest struggles. Despite our advancements, illness and imbalance seem to shadow our lives in ways rarely seen in the natural world. It is a fact that physical suffering is a universal experience that we witness all around and encounter within the confines of our human form. In contrast, animals roaming freely in the wild seldom suffer as humans do. Have you ever heard of a lion, monkey, or parrot grappling with high blood pressure, high cholesterol, a nervous breakdown, or heart failure? It is a different narrative once they are confined and stripped of their freedom; only then do they start developing health issues akin to our own.

The primary culprit behind the myriad mental and physical problems we grapple with today is the entanglement of our unconscious mind in an unconscious world. Stripped of our freedom of consciousness, we find ourselves bereft of the fundamental right to conscious thought. A prisoner of unconsciousness is the most significant kind of prisoner, and the death of consciousness represents the most profound demise. 'Die before you die' is not just a simple phrase; it holds a more straightforward meaning. The demise of excessive unconsciousness is all that is needed to attain freedom and liberation while still physically alive on earth. You harbour the power within to liberate yourself from the shackles of negativity right now, stepping into the realm of consciousness, where good health, success, joy, and prosperity eagerly await your arrival.

Meditation is the transformative key, a unique instrument capable of unlocking the gates of your mental prison and setting you free. To better understand how it works, we must first explore the inner workings of the mind itself.

The mind, by its nature, is repetitive, and negative thought patterns play on a loop like an auto-reverse player. When one cycle ends, another begins, creating a continuous loop. For instance, a thought of anger implants the seeds of vengeance in your unconscious mind; someone who has annoyed and disturbed your peace must face the consequences and punishment. This message is transmitted to the body cells, while your mental processes kick into action, and the thoughts persist until the desired outcome is achieved.

Consider this: who has the power to truly annoy you? It is typically someone close, someone you love, as a stranger can't enter your home and provoke anger. Nowadays, people go to great lengths to secure their properties, displaying signs like 'Trespassers will be prosecuted' or 'Beware of ferocious dogs.' Colonies and apartment buildings are fortified with security guards. Modern individuals take extensive precautions against strangers entering their domain without permission, yet they remain exposed, vulnerable, and often defenseless against those who are an integral part of their lives.

It is important to note that the part of you that feels hurt is not the heart, for the heart by its very nature is forgiving. It is also not the soul that radiates with compassion and unconditional love. So, what, then, causes so much pain? It is your ego—the false self, a distortion of your true self. A significant gap exists between the two, with the false part persistently being false, as it represents something you are not, while the true part remains authentic as the real you.

Now, let's look at the following question: In meditation, who assumes the role of the silent observer? It is the real you—the soul or spirit. And what is under observation? Everything that isn't you, and the ego is certainly not you as it is a false identity imposed unknowingly and will persist as long as you allow it to roam freely. The realisation of this absolute truth has the power to liberate you, shattering the chains of bondage.

In other words, meditation serves as a bridge back to reality, allowing your true self—consciousness—to take its rightful place as the observer, meticulously scrutinising the actions of your unconscious mind. When someone provokes you, and your reaction veers towards vengeance, your self-pride, your ego, feels wounded, leading you to believe that punishment is necessary. As a silent observer, you distinctly perceive the gap between action and reaction, often in the ratio of ten to one. The ego, smarting from the injury, seeks retribution, prompting you to devise ten different ways or reasons to hurt or punish the person who upset you. Amidst this mental turmoil, however, a single thought of forgiveness can arise. This is the gap between reaction and action, conscious and unconscious, and as a silent observer, you won't overlook it. You will also realise the profound truth that this single thought of forgiveness brings immense peace and happiness, whereas the ten unconscious thoughts of revenge cause tremendous strife, turbulence, and upheaval within your mental realm.

Forgiveness stands as our paramount virtue, a central

theme echoed by spiritual masters across diverse religions. Buddha, in his teachings, proclaimed, 'No matter the cause of your suffering, do not harm another, forgive them.' Jesus reiterated, 'Man should be forgiving, for as he forgives others, so will God forgive him.' Muhammad re-emphasised, 'God loves those who forgive their fellow beings.' Guru Nanak went a step further when he said, 'Countless people have perished without the spirit of forgiveness. Remove hatred from your mind; the whole world is your friend.'

Summarising these profound teachings on forgiveness, I have written a short poem that beautifully encapsulates its essence and significance:

If we truly wish to live,
Let us learn to forgive.
Life is meant to be lived,
To love and cherish,
The beauty of this world,
Love of every soul.

Why not be like the birds of the sea,
Who keep flying ceaselessly,
This earth isn't our final resting place,
We are here but momentarily,
Just to give our very best.

The secret of love,
Is to give and give,
If we truly wish to live,
Let us learn to forgive!

Meditation unfolds as the pathway to forgiveness, encompassing not only the ability to forgive others but also granting yourself forgiveness. To fathom the profound meaning of forgiveness, one must initially forgive oneself for past sins or unconscious actions. If you adhere to the belief that we are all sinners, the supreme form of repentance becomes forgiveness. God endows us with the ability to make U-turns, and forgiveness is precisely that—a U-turn. However, your unconscious mind may resist, perceiving the act as illicit and a challenge to its dominion.

It is vital to recognise that we are often at war with ourselves when it comes to forgiveness. This internal struggle arises because the mind, particularly the unconscious, clings to the past with fierce tenacity. Shaped by years of experience, conditioning, and perception, the unconscious mind holds memories and judgments, which are not merely recollections but seeds that continue to grow, influencing our present emotions, thoughts, and behaviours. When we hold on to these past wounds, we prevent ourselves from moving forward, tethered to the emotional weight of old grievances.

Thus, we can see how the unconscious mind resists forgiveness, mistaking it for condoning the very actions that caused suffering. But what, then, is the way forward? The truth we must realise is that forgiveness is not about condoning, excusing, or erasing the past. It is about releasing the emotional charge that continues to bind you to it. It is about choosing peace over pain. It is about recognising that the act of holding on to anger, resentment, and guilt only keeps you imprisoned. To forgive is to heal, to awaken, and to come home to the truth of who we are.

All in all, the act of forgiveness is a holistic practice, a process of dismantling the walls we build around our hearts and minds. When we forgive, we release not only the one who has wronged us but also ourselves, for we no longer allow the pain of the past to dictate our present reality. Put simply, forgiveness allows us to reclaim our power.

Awakening in the Eternal Now

Much of our inner struggle is tied to time—our minds dwell on the past, cling to regrets, or project guilt into an endless future. This becomes clear when we see that sin belongs to yesterday, while repentance seems to stretch into eternity. And this is why so many remain trapped in the past or future, whether through guilt or fear, and in doing so, deny themselves the possibility of growth and renewal.

This is why meditation becomes an indispensable tool, for its power lies in its ability to free us from the tyranny of time. The past, a fleeting echo, has already passed into oblivion, and the future, a realm of uncertainty, has yet to unfold. Both are mere illusions, shadows of what was and what may never be. It is only in the present moment, where the pulse of life beats in its fullness, that we find true freedom. Here, in this sacred now, we are whole, untouched by the ghosts of the past or the uncertainty of what lies ahead.

Through meditation, we have the opportunity to explore the void between yesterday and tomorrow, which is none other than today—the singular realm of existence. Today is the entirety of your possession, for it constitutes all that exists. Within this day, you can either sin, repent, or choose to awaken. Remember, awakening or enlightenment does not await us in the tomorrow. Instead, they stand at your very doorstep in this precise moment. All you must do is traverse the divide between yesterday and tomorrow.

Meditation serves as the bridge from which you can journey towards the gates of your personal heaven, within the realm of today—a realm where joy, love, peace, success, and prosperity eagerly await your embrace. Once more, the choice lies within your domain, for you are the master of your destiny. You can opt to enter your heaven today or defer it to an uncharted tomorrow that no living human being has ever glimpsed. And it is meditation that provides the key to unlocking the door to the present moment, where all things are possible. Through it, you awaken to the eternal truth: you are not bound by the past but liberated by the present.

In the next chapter, we will take a deeper dive into how we can remain anchored in the present moment and cultivate a life of awareness, peace, and inner freedom.

Chapter 7
Returning to the Present

The Eternal Call to Honour the Present

In the enchanting tapestry of wisdom, a venerable teacher once wove these words: 'Take therefore no thought for tomorrow; for tomorrow shall take thought for the things of itself. Sufficient for the day is the evil of not doing what should be done.' This timeless counsel holds profound relevance in the modern labyrinth we navigate. Its essence is simple yet powerful: refrain from brooding over the quandaries of tomorrow, as tomorrow will carry its own burdens and tribulations. What truly hinders us today is the neglect of present responsibilities—the squandering of precious moments in worry about challenges that are yet to arrive.

It is remarkable how this call to honour the present moment has been reiterated by visionaries throughout the ages. Kabir Das, the illustrious Indian poet and religious reformer of the fourteenth century, gave us an enduring axiom: *'Kal kare so aaj kar, aaj kare so abh. Pal mein pralaya ho jayegi, phir karogay kabh?'* In English, it echoes, 'What you have to do tomorrow, do it today, what you have to do today, do it now. In a moment, death may arrive, so when will you do what you have to do?' These words reverberate a parallel sentiment with an identical imperative.

For many, the elusive dance of happiness often masquerades in the attire of tomorrow. It is envisioned as a distant companion, entwined with specific conditions. How familiar are the refrains, 'I will be happy when I accumulate a certain wealth, possess a bigger house, drive a Mercedes-Benz, adorn myself with a diamond necklace, attain a particular societal stature, secure a promotion at work, witness my children's matrimony, or the day I retire.' Do these words not resonate in the corridors of society and, perhaps, in the chambers of your own aspirations as prerequisites for happiness? The key insight here is that they all share a common thread—each one tied to a tomorrow, a distant horizon, that has yet to arrive.

In the enigmatic realms of tomorrow, a shadow of unease and yearning for a better existence often shrouds the mind, leading one into the clutches of acute unconsciousness. Moreover, a significant portion of humankind, already steeped in a ninety per cent unconscious state, resorts to substances like alcohol or drugs, further draining the meager ten per cent of consciousness they possess. For such people, the constant preoccupation with future thoughts and worries seems enough to sustain them. Yet, freedom from this cycle is always within reach. By learning to release the grip of tomorrow and awaken to the power of the present, we can reclaim our full awareness and live with greater peace and clarity. In this chapter, we will learn how to cultivate that presence and open the way to a more conscious and fulfilling life.

The Power of the Present Moment

Time is undeniably an essential facet of our lives, always racing forward. And while time stands as our most abundant possession, paradoxically, people often lament, 'I wish I had more time.' Although time is indeed our most invaluable asset, it has transformed into our greatest liability due to the gross mismanagement perpetrated by our unconscious minds. What we overlook is that this very moment is our time. It belongs to us, and no one can seize it except us. The truly successful understand this truth: that achievement comes from investing their complete, conscious effort into the present, the sole moment at their disposal.

Pete Sampras, an icon in the world of tennis, held dominion over the sport for well over a decade. The number of years he spent as the world's top-ranked player during that era was unparalleled. His matches were a spectacle, filled with miraculous and unbelievable shots that left audiences in a state of sheer astonishment for days. Even when he erred on the first serve, his second serve manifested as an ace, a feat deemed the most formidable in tennis. And while most players tend to adopt a cautious approach on their second serve, striving to avert the risk of a double fault, Pete Sampras boldly defied this trend. His monumental concentration epitomised a state of complete presence in the current moment. In his world, the present moment was the only reality, and he harnessed it to secure victory upon victory. This profound approach underpins the success of champions across various fields, be it sports, acting, business, or any other endeavour. They understand the present moment is a gift and skillfully utilise it to their advantage.

The flip side, however, is living entangled in psychological time, where unconsciousness drives us to see the world only through the shadows of the past or the anxieties of the future. People, including parents, who often reminisce about the superiority of their bygone era compared to today, have a habit of asserting that education, music, movies, and human values were all superior then. This cycle of nostalgia continues as these parents' children grow up and in turn, repeat similar claims to their offspring. This cycle of repetitiveness seems virtually endless.

Upon careful observation of your thought patterns within your mind, you will discern their remarkable repetitiveness. Furthermore, you will recognise that these thoughts invariably relate to either the past, a time long gone, or the future, a time yet to come. What becomes glaringly evident is that, irrespective of whether your thoughts dwell in the past or the future, they transpire in the present moment. A more prominent truth that you may inadvertently overlook is this: if your present remains consumed by the past or future, are you not squandering this moment, the most exquisite 'present' at your disposal? Consider, for instance, if during a tennis match, Pete Sampras had occupied his thoughts with past triumphs or the upcoming Wimbledon or US Open, what might have ensued? He could have very well missed the present match and the opportunity for victory, along with the accompanying applause.

Exiting the realm of psychological time is not an arduous task; it necessitates heightened presence in the present moment. The instant you grasp this truth, you can initiate the process. Should you waste your present moments ruminating about the past or being anxious about the future, you are, in fact, doing so in the here and now. Will this aid you in any manner? Can your past or future alter your present circumstances? Certainly not, but they can undoubtedly worsen them.

This doesn't mean the past or the future are inherently harmful. The past can be a sagacious teacher, illuminating the missteps you might have taken. If your thoughts often meander through the corridors of the past, unearth those misjudgements, for they cast a direct influence on your present state. Reflecting upon and amending them can elevate your awareness and consciousness, ensuring you do not reenact them today. Much akin to a meticulous athlete who dissects matches or events where they faltered, then invests boundless hours perfecting their craft to emerge as a champion, you too harbour the capability to be the champion of your life, gleaning wisdom from past missteps. So, if you have devoted a considerable portion of your existence to ruminating on the past, now is the chance to rectify and redeem those unconscious thoughts.

The same principle extends to the future. If daydreams of a brighter tomorrow have dominated a significant expanse of your time, it is time to awaken from this dreamlike stupor. It mirrors the wake-up call delivered by many great sages and saints. Yet, the majority of humankind expends minimal effort in deciphering the profound meaning concealed within these divine, mystical words, while continuing to persist in a state of unconscious slumber.

A similar sentiment is also echoed by several scriptures that illuminate the fundamental reality of the relationship between God and man with the resounding phrase, 'I am that I am.' These words hold great significance as they direct us to an eternal truth: I am that I am in this present moment, untouched by the tethers of yesterday or tomorrow. They point directly to the timeless essence of our existence on earth in this boundless universe, liberated from the shackles of psychological time and unburdened by past or future, as it stretches infinitely.

The reality is that in our quest for control over the passage of time, we crafted the clock and metamorphosed into mechanical entities in this time-bound world. This transition has distanced us from our authentic nature, the nature of God. If the very essence of the Creator's being is encapsulated in the phrase 'I am that I am,' then how can we deviate from this truth? We exist precisely as we are in this present moment—nothing more, nothing less. And our sole opponent, which prevents us from realising this truth, is our unconscious mind, which has seemingly clinched victory throughout. Not because it is superior, but because our own shortcomings have permitted it to reign. Only upon grasping this fundamental verity can one initiate earnest endeavours to rectify the conspicuous imbalance and ascend to higher states of consciousness. To be conscious is to remain cognisant of and face the unblemished reality of the present moment, for it is the most invaluable possession at your disposal. What you have to do tomorrow, do it today; the work of today, do it right now; or else, the present moment will wither away.

Inhale the Future, Exhale the Past

Having reflected on the power of the present, we now turn to practice. The meditation process elucidated in the preceding chapter is not merely theory; it unfolds as a potent tool for deepening awareness. Even twenty minutes of conscious practise can attune you to the present moment and your inner state.

To experience this directly, let us embark on a brief meditational experiment by revisiting that process. Close your eyes and take seven deliberate deep breaths. Consciously feel each inhalation as if originating from your abdomen, ascending through your chest, and exiting through your nostrils.

Now, shift your focus to the breath entering through your nostrils, descending through your chest towards your abdomen, then ascending from your abdomen through your chest, and exiting through your nostrils. Observe this sequence for a few moments, and you will recognise the authentic process of breathing. Each breath flows into the body through the nostrils towards the abdomen and flows out in the opposite direction, creating a rhythmic cycle—an orchestration and affirmation of life's ceaseless vitality.

If you can now perceive this rhythmic flow, you are awakening to the true essence of your life. Each inhalation ushers in the future, while each exhalation transforms into the past, and the breaths within you signify your present. The entire dance of breath shapes a perfect circle; every moment the future evolves into the present, and the present transmutes into the past. Within this perpetual cycle resides your very being. Life pulses through you because of the breaths of the present; the future breathes life into you, while the past dies every moment.

Another important thing to notice is the fleeting pause or gap that exists between inhalation and exhalation. Gently close your eyes once again, inhale and exhale, while endeavouring to sense this gap and understand its significance. This will take you closer to profound realisation that all we possess is this gap, which is the present moment. The gap between inhaling and exhaling is the threshold separating the past and the future. We can't even grip it, for it is a mere void or vacuum between opposing forces—in and out, past and future, life and death, consciousness and unconsciousness.

This gap conceals the enigma of our cosmic evolution and life on earth because it embodies all that genuinely exists. Your presence in this very moment is your authentic identity, emancipated from the cycle of death and birth. Neither the future nor the present ensnares it—the present moment is the sole realm of existence, the eternal verity that has been, is, and always shall be. And when we truly claim the authority to inhabit this moment and experience the truth of our existence, we come to realise the eternal wisdom: 'I am that I am.'

But the greatest obstacle on this journey is our need to cling to life. Can you clasp your breath? If you allow the incoming breath to enter but deny its departure, what will unfold? You must relinquish it or brace for suffocation and eventual demise, as you cannot clasp it. Put simply, we cannot seize the incoming future and the departing past simultaneously. The future swiftly unfurls into the present and transmutes into the past, and we cannot cling to any, neither the future nor the past. Thus, we can look at life as a continuous flowing river, ever-moving and alive only when allowed to run its natural course.

The Middle Way to Superconsciousness

Up to this point, we have explored how the mind drifts endlessly between past regrets and future anxieties. Yet there exists a higher state, one that transcends both extremes. The state of superconsciousness resides precisely at the midpoint between consciousness and unconsciousness—a realm suspended between yesterday and tomorrow. In truth, reaching this middle ground is far more natural than it seems. Just as a soccer game commences from the middle, the grand play of life also unfurls from this central point. To witness reality as it is, look closely at the ongoing matches within your mental kingdom between the following teams. The sole rule is to watch these games as a neutral spectator, free from favouritism. In essence, just be a true sports lover who is there to revel in the game, to cheer, to laud the victor.

- Team Desire versus Team Fulfillment
- Team Anger versus Team Happiness
- Team Attachment versus Team Detachment
- Team Greed versus Team Generosity
- Team Ego versus Team Humility

As you transition into the role of a silent observer in the intricate game of life, perceiving these contests from an impartial vantage, you will unlock the divine facets of your nature and delve into the genuine wonders of happiness, contentment, and bliss. Positioned as a neutral spectator amidst desire-fulfillment, anger-happiness, attachment-detachment, greed-generosity, ego-humility, you will be in the middle, witnessing their dynamics. You will then discover that desire ushers in unease, while fulfillment brings tranquility; anger ignites fervor, and happiness maintains composure; attachment fosters materialism, detachment steers towards spiritualism; greed causes both you and others to bleed, yet generosity annihilates the seeds of destruction; ego veers you towards shortsightedness, whereas humility ushers in enlightenment.

Isn't it straightforward to inhabit the midpoint and observe the game of life as a silent, impartial spectator? These matches unfold ceaselessly, enacted in the inner recesses of your mind. No need to squander time seeking the matches of yesteryear or planning for tomorrow's games, allow yourself all the time in the world to relish the thrill and drama right now—in this present moment.

Moreover, to stand at the centre as a true aficionado of the ongoing contests between consciousness and unconsciousness is the state of superconsciousness. Gautama Buddha's sagacious counsel to attain peace and be victorious in the battle of life was to follow the middle way, and this is that way. The truth is, there are no genuine winners or vanquished, there never were, and there never will be. Simply revel in this game of creation by remaining present, moment to moment, and bask in the bliss of eternity. The garden is here, heaven is here, and the kingdom of God exists within your very essence—in your 'I am that I am,' and not in 'I was' or 'I will be.'

Chapter 8

THE SUPERCONSCIOUS STATE

From Bondage to Freedom

IN THE REALM OF SUFI NARRATIVES, WHERE MEANINGS run deep and truths are wrapped in metaphor, a captivating tale unfolds—a tale that transcends the boundaries of comprehension, pointing towards the profound realities of life, death, religion, and the intricate dance of traditions that shape our earthly journey.

In the bygone days, there existed three brothers—Aryan, Iqbal, and Gyan—each on a quest for truth, charting their unique courses through the labyrinth of existence. Aryan, the contemplative, would immerse himself in ceaseless thought until his head pulsated with the weight of introspection. Iqbal, the yogi, assumed postures connecting earth and sky until even his head bowed under the strain. Gyan, the seeker of knowledge, delved into books, thinking and contemplating until his head, too, ached with the pursuit. Despite the passage of years, the elusive truth remained a distant horizon.

In their quest for resolution, the brothers sought counsel from a renowned sage, who prescribed a remedy: meditate for an hour each morning, afternoon, and evening for twenty-one days. Upon completing this regimen, each brother dreamt of the truth they sought. Aryan envisioned a land of fools as his destination, Iqbal glimpsed a magic mirror in a land of mirrors reflecting the truth, and Gyan dreamt of Jinn in a village called Whirlpool, the revealer of his sought-after truth. Armed with these dreams, the trio embarked on their individual odysseys.

After enduring days of travel and hardship, Aryan stumbled upon the land of fools. The peculiarities of the inhabitants left him astounded. He first encountered a woman, labouring under the weight of a heavy door upon her head. Inquiring about her destination and offering assistance, he was met with the explanation, 'This morning, as my husband left for work, he instructed me not to let anyone pass this door, for he brought home bricks of gold yesterday. I am now en route to the marketplace for groceries, taking the door along to ward off intruders.'

As Aryan ventured deeper, more surprises awaited him. He then met with a group of terrified individuals staring in dread at a sizable watermelon, gleaming in the morning sunlight. Upon questioning the cause of their fear, they responded, 'We have never witnessed such a monster. It will grow bigger and eventually annihilate us.' Offering to dispel their fears with the truth, Aryan was met with a resolute refusal: 'No, no, no! We don't want to know anything. Just kill it if you can.'

Without hesitation, Aryan unsheathed his knife, sliced the reddish fruit, and began to eat. Witnessing this astonishing act, the fools erupted in exclamation, 'Our saviour, our lord, the messenger of God has come. He has slain the demon and consumed its blood.' The news spread, drawing a multitude of onlookers. Some reverently touched his feet, seeking blessings, while others observed in disbelief. Overnight, Aryan ascended to fame in the land of fools.

Determined to impart truth, he devoted his life to teaching the fools that he was an ordinary person like them, possessing two eyes, two legs, two arms, and a heart. After years of diligent teaching, Aryan eventually uncovered the truth he sought. Although the fools gained some understanding through his efforts, the profound truth remained elusive to them, despite his unwavering endeavours.

Iqbal, too, embarked on an extensive journey before discovering the magic mirror in the land of mirrors. Suspended in an ancient, abandoned well by a delicate thread, it appeared diminutive amidst the array of large and medium-sized mirrors that adorned the land. Puzzled by its title, Iqbal's curiosity piqued and upon gazing into it, he immediately found the truth he sought. Much like Aryan, he resolved to dedicate his life to the people of this land, intending to share the profound revelation he had experienced in that instant. Despite years of strenuous efforts, he passed away without successfully imparting his truth. While the people gained awareness of the mirror's various uses, their understanding remained confined to its surface.

Gyan, similar to Aryan and Iqbal, set out on an arduous quest to find the village of Whirlpool and encounter the enigmatic individual named Jinn. After traversing numerous days, he finally located Jinn, who upon inquiry about the truth, responded, 'I see you have journeyed far and delved into many books in pursuit of your quest. Now, follow the instructions I shall provide, and you will reach your destination.' Gyan received directions to recite specific phrases sequentially, sing uplifting songs, adopt particular postures, and perform a series of unique actions.

Gyan initiated his pursuit with resolute commitment, practising the designated phrases, songs, postures, and actions diligently. After years of tireless effort, he finally uncovered the truth he sought. Following in the footsteps of Aryan and Iqbal, he decided to dedicate his life to the people of Whirlpool, intending to share his divine discovery. For several years, he imparted the practised phrases, songs, postures, and actions. While many became adept, excelling in chanting, singing, posturing, or performing unique actions, none grasped the truth he had uncovered.

Does this narrative not echo the complexities of our existence? Are we not the descendants of Aryan, Iqbal, and Gyan's disciples? The watermelon still looms large, the monster specter very much alive; we spill the blood of animals and humans alike in broad daylight. Mirrors, not confined to one but adorning every room, have become an integral part of our homes, adhering to the belief that bigger is indeed better. A mirror serves as an unfiltered reflection of our essence. If anger courses through us, the mirror mirrors that anger; if laughter resonates, the mirror reflects that laughter. Yet, do we truly perceive the emotions behind the reflection? A mirror, in its unadulterated reality, holds the truth we yearn for, but can we decipher it? The recitation of phrases, the chanting of mantras, the melody of devotional songs, and the rhythm of prayers persist in our lives like a well-rehearsed performance, and the postures and mechanised actions unfold repetitively, akin to the encore of a renowned play or a captivating spectacle.

Despite this, are we any nearer to the truth? We are still on a quest, pursuing what Aryan, Iqbal, and Gyan discovered many years ago. Our failure lies in clinging to the methods they left behind while neglecting to seek what they themselves discovered.

In the same vein, Buddha, Jesus, Muhammad, and Guru Nanak uncovered their personal truths, which they actively sought and discovered. Contrary to the misconception that they were born enlightened, they traversed the troubles and tribulations of life, transcending the barriers of the body and mind to attain the state of superconsciousness. Both Jesus and Guru Nanak achieved enlightenment at thirty after years of toil, Muhammad at forty-two, and Buddha spent numerous years in the wilderness, reaching the pinnacle of consciousness at thirty-five. If they were inherently enlightened, why did they not embark on their missions of preaching and healing earlier? Had they all commenced their endeavours at a uniform age of twenty, one might concede that they were indeed the chosen ones, God's special messengers, bringing his word and message to us.

From this emerges an undeniable truth: we are all the chosen ones. Would a father bestow greater powers upon one child and fewer upon others? Have you ever encountered individuals with four eyes, four legs, two hearts, and three minds? God has not differentiated among us in physical attributes, so how can we designate a select few as chosen and dismiss the rest as undeserving? The only realm where God exercised discretion was the human mind, an act born out of deep love for his creation. It granted us full access to explore creative potential, traverse freedom of expression, and exhibit individuality in thought and action. It was not His intention for us to behave like robots or preprogrammed inventions, so He could play with us as He pleased. We received complete freedom of thought, expression, and action—the freedom to desire or not to desire, to remain in bondage or slavery, or to set ourselves free.

Buddha, Jesus, Muhammad, and Guru Nanak masterfully wielded their freedom of thought, expression, and action, meticulously crafting their destinies. Much like the trio in our narrative—Aryan, Iqbal, and Gyan—they toiled on the intricate journey of self-discovery, surmounting barriers and navigating hurdles to harmonise the unconscious and conscious forces of the mind. In this intricate dance, they ascended to the pinnacle of superconsciousness, a transcendent state opening the window to the divine and the door to God's eternal realm. Here, they confronted the stark reality of their existence and discerned their place in the vast expanse of the universe. And once these enlightened souls unearthed the profound truths about themselves, the unfolding of their earthly missions commenced. Each, in their distinctive manner, chose to bestow the acquired wisdom upon their fellow beings, tailoring their teachings to the unique zeitgeist of the eras they inhabited.

A meticulous examination of the teachings of these spiritual luminaries reveals a rich tapestry of commonalities. Their collective guidance converges on the imperative of awakening, of conscious acknowledgment of the unconscious, breaking free from the shackles of tradition and division, and undergoing a rebirth to reunite with one's genuine nature. In essence, their wisdom points us toward the same destination—the awakening of our true self and the freedom to live in harmony with it.

The Eternal Celebration of Life

After exploring the nature of consciousness and the call to awakening, it becomes clear that life reveals its deepest truths not in complexity, but in simplicity. The moment you begin to celebrate life in its present, unadorned form, wisdom flows like a torrent. This earth, fashioned as God's playground, is a realm for our play—an arena where each day unfolds as an opportunity to revel in existence. It is an invitation to acknowledge and marvel at this human form, the greatest miracle in itself.

The Bhagavad Gita, a revered scripture of India, encapsulates this truth and the law of existence with eloquence: 'Why worry, and whom or what do you fear? Who can harm or kill you? You are the eternal soul beyond birth and death. Everything that has happened, is happening, and will happen unfolds for your ultimate good. Do not dwell on the past nor fret about the future; live in the present and savor each moment.

What have you lost, and why grieve? You brought nothing into this world, and you will leave with nothing. Everything you gained or lost happened here. You arrived empty-handed, and one day you will depart the same way—not even a tiny needle can be carried along. What is yours today belonged to someone else before and will belong to someone else tomorrow. The material possessions, relations, and the related feelings of contentment that you claim as yours are the authentic sources of your suffering.

Change is the essence of life. What you perceive as death is, in fact, a new beginning. In one moment, you become an emperor; in the next, you turn into a beggar. Remove negative thoughts like yours and mine, ours and theirs, my religion and your religion, and you will realise the truth—that all belongs to you, and you belong to all.

This body isn't yours, and you don't belong to it. It is composed of fire, water, air, earth, and space, and will dissolve into these at your physical death. Only the soul is eternal, and part of the supreme soul we call God. The soul belongs to the timeless world, free from the cycle of death and birth. Understanding this truth grants freedom from worries, fears, sufferings, and sorrow, transcending past and future, yesterday and tomorrow.'

Could there be a more profound expression or description of the truth and law of existence than these words? Though we all belong to an eternal, timeless realm, we have become time-bound due to ignorance of our real identity. While we celebrate birth with joy and happiness, but mourn death with tears and sadness, missing the most significant fact. With every moment, a new breath is born to sustain our life, while the departing breath fades away forever. Do we ever mourn that? The true essence of our existence is that with every breath we are being born eternally. Put simply, every exhale is a small death and every inhale is a new birth. This is the essence of life, of existence, unfolding in its purest form.

So, why not live and celebrate this timeless birth in alignment with our eternal nature? Why not recognise that the fleeting moments of joy and sorrow we experience are merely transient reflections of a deeper, undying reality? When we awaken to this truth, we begin to understand that the limitations we impose upon ourselves are constructs of the mind, driven by the illusion of time. Birth and death, joy and sorrow, are simply different manifestations of the same eternal process—the dance of the soul in this temporal world.

To live in alignment with this truth is to embrace each breath as a sacred gift, a continuous unfolding of our true self. In fact, we need not wait for some far-off moment of enlightenment or transcendence. It is in the simple act of breathing, of being present, that we connect with the eternal. By celebrating the miracle of each moment, we free ourselves from the chains of attachment to time. We transcend the cycle of birth and death, understanding that we are, in essence, neither bound by nor defined by them. In embracing the present as an eternal birth, we return to the fullness of our divine nature, aligning with the infinite peace and wisdom that resides within us.

Moreover, by living in harmony with this truth, we can let go of our fears and anxieties, knowing that we are forever reborn in each moment, forever part of the eternal flow of existence. Our true identity is not bound to the fleeting physical form, but to the soul that transcends the limits of time and space. It is this understanding that brings freedom, joy, and peace—an awakening to the eternal nature of life itself.

Once this realisation dawns, the celebration of life no longer waits for grand occasions. Instead, it becomes a constant, intimate recognition of our own divinity. And truly, there is no prescribed method for celebration, no need for elaborate preparations. It is not akin to a religious ceremony marking the birth of Buddha, Jesus, Muhammad, or Guru Nanak. As mentioned, your rebirth is a continuous phenomenon, happening every moment. To celebrate this ongoing birth, simply revel in the essence of your true nature. Undoubtedly, this incredible human form has been bestowed upon you for a specific purpose.

In this celebration, you are not simply living for the sake of living. You are existing for the highest purpose—to bring forth your innate greatness, to serve, to create, and to love. When we attune to this higher calling, we begin to see that the essence of joy is not confined to humans alone but resonates throughout all of creation. Even animals, free in the jungles, celebrate. They follow the cycle of existence, staying clear of human maladies, living in peace with themselves and their creator. However, when caged, they lose all that, becoming akin to us. We, too, can liberate ourselves from the cage of ignorance and embark on this process of celebration by embracing our day-to-day and moment-to-moment cycle of existence.

So, upon waking in the morning, celebrate the dawn of a new day. While lying still in bed, tune into the rhythmic dance of your breath and embrace the sheer joy of being alive. As you rise, maintain this connection by sporting a constant smile, whether it is the simple act of washing your face, brushing your teeth, or engaging in any routine. During your morning bath, allow the water to cascade over you like a refreshing natural waterfall. Be fully present, steering clear of thoughts about breakfast or looming problems. Those can be addressed later—right now, immerse yourself in the moment and enjoy a truly refreshing bath.

Avoid the hurried pace that drags you away from the beauty of the present. A simple remedy is to wake up an hour earlier than your usual time. As you navigate through your morning routine, maintain your presence and inner joy. When indulging in the first meal of the day, relish every single morsel, letting your taste buds revel in the ecstasy of a date, mango, coconut, or an exotic sandwich. Experience the timeless joys found in the overflowing nectars of eternity.

Maintain that perpetual smile as it significantly contributes to being joyful and fully present in all your endeavours. Strive to mirror the conscientiousness of a pregnant woman, unmatched in her care and presence. Whether walking, rising, bathing, eating, or contemplating thoughts, her caution is profound. Why such meticulousness during pregnancy? It is because she feels the truth within—the continuous vibration of the unborn child, alive, kicking, and breathing. While she may not be as conscious about her own life post-delivery, her sole concern now is the life within. So be pregnant with the truth within, genuinely concerned with the life inside, and revel in the joy of being alive, celebrating the eternal existence of your true nature within this human form.

As you progress through the day, immerse yourself entirely in the present. Embrace your children and spouse with hugs and kisses when leaving and returning home. The significance of a hug can never be emphasised enough; it is the sweetest treat you can offer to your loved ones. In moments of misunderstanding or challenges, a hug possesses the power to liberate spirits and brighten the day. Never shy away from this simple yet profound gesture. It washes away poison, illuminates the heart, ignites the soul, bringing you closer to the divine essence and the warmth of home. A hug is a splendid gift, extending not only to others but also to your own body and soul.

If driving to work, relish the joy as if driving for the first time in your life. While at work, strive for that perpetual state of joy and happiness. Do not merely work for the sake of working, and never perceive a problem as an insurmountable obstacle. Do your best and resolve it joyfully. Even if met with initial setbacks, savour the joy of trial and error, akin to the persistent spider that keeps trying until it succeeds. Every failure is a stride towards success, so relish failures as much as triumphs, focusing solely on your current actions. Additionally, do not seek external validation or rewards; the joy of engaging in your endeavours with happiness is the ultimate reward.

During lunchtime, intentionally disconnect from work for at least thirty minutes. Delve into the flavours of your food, savouring each morsel, being entirely present in the moment. Let go of work-related concerns, immersing yourself completely in the current activity. Such mindful mealtimes will rejuvenate you, returning to work with enthusiasm and readiness to tackle the excitement and challenges of the contemporary world.

As you make your way home in the evening, sustain the joy of being and presence in continuous motion. Return with the same enthusiasm as if you were coming back from a long, joyful journey. Greet your loved ones with hugs and kisses as if reuniting after an extended separation. Leave work-related issues on the table, treating them as if they cease to exist in the sanctuary of your home. Once home, let the feeling of being alive persist. Spend quality time with your children. Discern their needs and how you can offer support. Whether a father or a mother, be their close friend, stepping into their shoes and reliving the innocent magic of your own childhood. Refrain from dictating or judging and ensure that, as they grow, you won't face a repetition of oppressive scenarios. Instead, plant the seeds of unconditional love in their tender hearts, and as they blossom into strong individuals, you will undoubtedly reap the bountiful rewards.

When your favourite TV show, sports event, or the latest romance or action movie takes the stage, immerse yourself fully as if you were watching it live. Laugh freely when amusement strikes, shed tears if moved by an emotional scene. Hold nothing back, for clinging means embracing a form of death. Every demise, whether of the physical body, ego, or the passing moment, is a form of mourning. Therefore, refuse to mourn. Remember that life is a continuous celebration of your timeless existence, an invitation to love and be loved in its entirety, in an utterly unconditional manner.

Dinner holds its sacred moment. Once again, relish every morsel on your table. Engage your senses—taste the flavours, inhale the aroma of the ingredients in your favourite dish. Chew deliberately, about thirty-two times, as it is a profoundly healthy practice. By doing so, you extend the enjoyment of your meal, fortify your teeth, evade cavities and unnecessary dental bills, and lighten the load on your digestive system. It is akin to winning four games with one stroke—you revel in the taste longer, your teeth get stronger, and digestion is expedited, and collectively these acts enhance the joys of the journey of life.

When the moment for romance unfolds, let it become a distinctive occasion. Stepping into the bedroom sanctuary with your beloved, immerse yourself completely in the present. Acknowledge the paramount significance of this moment as it transcends a mere interlude. This is a golden opportunity to articulate love beyond the confines of mere words and thoughts. Let this be a nostalgic journey, a chance to revisit the boundless exuberance of teenage love, capturing the very essence of falling in love at that tender and enthralling age. Allow the room to be filled with the magic of shared emotions, an intimate dance of hearts intertwined in the celebration of love.

How enchanting could your day be, beginning with the dawn, celebrations starting the moment you wake, and continuing from one moment to the next? As the day progresses, you remain present and alive in all your actions and words. The day starts with a romantic embrace, with a love of your own presence, and concludes with a similar romanticism, the joy of being awake in bed with your beloved partner. Falling asleep, you anticipate waking up to yet another day to celebrate your journey of life. Even if you do not awaken, the departing soul carries no regrets of not having fully lived or enjoyed every moment on earth.

Does this proposition appear daunting? Is there any hindrance to embracing such a celebration? This is your life, a manifestation of the joy of being alive, and each moment is worthy of celebration. The inherent beauty of life, when viewed through a lens of gratitude, beckons us to celebrate it, not only in moments of triumph but also in the quiet, seemingly mundane acts that unfold daily. Every breath we inhale, every step we take, is an opportunity to acknowledge the miracle of our existence. And yet, many of us go through life as though it were an endless to-do list, failing to pause and revel in the sheer act of being alive.

What, then, is this academic accolade we dub a Master of Business Administration (MBA)? At its core, it stands as an educational journey and training ground, shaping you into a master of time management, equipping you with skills to navigate the complexities of the modern world, and ensuring success in your professional pursuits. The MBA curriculum delves into the intricacies of programming your day-to-day activities, honing the ability to distinguish between the important, the urgent, and the insignificant, and fostering the capacity to be fully present in every task. Yet, it is not just about managing time in an efficient manner; it is about mastering the art of awareness and presence, both within the professional realm and beyond.

In simple terms, attaining the state of superconsciousness parallels the journey of acquiring an MBA. It necessitates learning and honing your mind in the art of time management, nurturing the ability to concentrate and be present in all endeavours, whether they pertain to work or leisure. So, as you embark on this transformative journey, your dedication extends to delivering your utmost to yourself, to the nourishment you provide your body, to the tasks you undertake, to the individuals you encounter, and above all, to your family, your well-being, and the cultivation of inner wealth. This inner wealth stands as the sole enduring facet that seamlessly integrates with our being, carried forward as we conclude our earthly sojourn.

This truth is poignantly encapsulated in these sacred verses, 'Lay not up for yourselves treasures upon earth, where moth and rust corrupt, and where thieves break through and steal. But lay up for yourselves treasures in heaven, where neither moth nor rust corrupts, and where thieves do not break through nor steal.' The message resounds that what we accumulate in the material realm will fade, but the treasure of the soul—the love, wisdom, and compassion we cultivate—endures beyond our lifetime.

The Final Awakening

Once we begin to awaken to the deeper truths of existence, our understanding of life and the world around us starts to shift profoundly. Even as we recognise the inevitability of the physical body's demise, this should not deter us from celebrating life or striving for growth, perfection, and purpose. Over time, the ultimate reality of our existence within this astonishing Universe gradually reveals itself—a realisation that we are all transient visitors on Earth, journeying through evolution and growth with a visa stamped with a predetermined expiration date. Earth is not our final home; it is a temporary sojourn, a platform to graduate from this school of life by sowing the seeds of love.

The secret to a fulfilled life lies in the principles of love and forgiveness entwined in the cosmic law of sow and reap. Let us earnestly learn and practice the art of love, acknowledging the profound truth that I belong to you, you belong to me, and love is the universal bond that binds us all. Undoubtedly, love stands as the most resolute teacher, and the world would unequivocally be a happier place if we recognised that hatred impoverishes us rather than enriches.

Moreover, the pervasive misery and pain in our surroundings serve as a reflection of our collective actions; we have constructed these divisions and factions. It is high time to dismantle the barriers that obscure our vision of unity, irrespective of race, colour, and religion. To attain perfection, we need nothing more than each other's affection. This simple, yet profound truth is at the heart of every tradition, every philosophy, and every path of spiritual awakening. It is not the accolades or the material possessions we accumulate that determine our worth, but the love we share, the kindness we extend, and the peace we nurture within. By cultivating these values, we fulfill our true purpose and contribute to the collective good of all humanity.

If you encounter obstacles in breaking down these barriers—human-made or otherwise—to free yourself from the shackles of ignorance and reach states of perfection, idealism, and superconsciousness, consider how figures like Buddha, Jesus, Muhammad, and Guru Nanak have illuminated the path. They have shown us how to sow the seeds of love and guide ourselves towards that elevated state. The sole disparity between them and us lies in the fact that they actively planted those seeds, harmonising the unconscious and conscious forces of desire, ego, anger, greed, and lust. In contrast, we find ourselves holding onto those seeds, sitting idle and hopeful for their return, anticipating the day of awakening, Qayamat, salvation, or some unknown revolution.

Similarly, the ancient scriptures of both the East and the West unveil a unique yet straightforward path to rouse from unconsciousness, ascend to heightened awareness, and attain the pinnacle of superconsciousness. In elucidating this journey, I will employ a poet's heart to articulate an enlightening message on how we can transition from our present condition to attain that sublime state and become one with all creation.

How Do We Go There from Here?

That place where we will find eternal bliss,
Love as sweet as the first warm, tender kiss.
How do we go there from here?
The shortest, straightforward route is,
Let's turn back time to that innocent age,
And become kids again.

Once more, let our hearts be brimmed,
With love and laughter,
Only childhood can bring.
God, too, is a child and revels in play,
From sorrow and hatred, he stays away.
As children, we are fascinated with all life brings,

Yet, as we mature,
We cast aside those adventures and thrills.

Ego and pride supplant the love and laughter we once had,
The odyssey from a child to an adult,
Often takes a disheartening clad.
God resides where the child is,
How do we go there from here?
Let's turn back time to that innocent age,
And become kids again.

So, let's turn back the hands of time and rediscover the purity and innocence of our childhood days. In that pristine state, a child mirrors the purity of the divine, their heart brimming with unconditional love, and a perpetual joyful smile adorning their face. In the scriptures of the East, this profound truth reflects through the enchanting tales of Krishna's childhood, unveiling a portrayal of unparalleled purity, carefree exuberance, wisdom, fearlessness, and a divine spirit persisting throughout his formative years.

And if we shift our focus towards the scriptures of the West, we find a similar essence of enlightenment or superconsciousness revealed through these words of Jesus: 'Unless you change and become like little children, you cannot enter the kingdom of heaven.' Every child is endowed with an untainted heart and an unrestricted spirit, free from the confines of any religious doctrine or fear of the unknown. Operating perpetually in a natural state of learning, children navigate life through trial and experimentation. Engrossed in their current pursuits, they are fueled by genuine joy and purpose, blissfully detached from the outcome. At this juncture, it is not work but an immersive experience—a delightful game of life where complete focus, unwavering dedication, and an insatiable spirit to learn and explore harmonise with ease and wonder. Likewise, Guru Nanak bestowed upon humankind the wisdom to become lifelong learners, echoing the literal meaning of a Sikh as 'learner'—one who, akin to a child, remains open and eager to learn at all times.

Once you transition into this state of perpetual learning, engaging in the game of life with a childlike spirit, you undergo a transformative metamorphosis. You cease to be just an individual; you evolve into a Buddha, Jesus, Mohammed, Krishna, or Guru Nanak. It is in this state that the divine purpose underlying creation and your authentic place in this incredible universe gradually unfold. Then the mystery of existence with all its splendours and wonders radiates through your body, mind, and soul, illuminating you with boundless light. This becomes your gateway to enlightenment, nirvana, awakening, salvation, or superconsciousness—a state where all belongs to you, and you, in turn, belong to all.

Yet, reaching this sublime state requires dedication and conscious effort. Schools that integrate the essential principles of inner science outlined in this work—encompassing the body, mind, and soul—create a rare environment for transformative learning, uniting parents, teachers, and pupils in mutual growth. Through meaningful discussions at home and in school, these principles become pillars of shared understanding. Children naturally exist in a pure state, often likened to a kingdom of heaven, yet parental influences can unintentionally impose limitations inherited from previous generations. Thus, it becomes essential to reflect deeply on fundamental beliefs surrounding marriage, love, religion, spirituality, customs, traditions, and self-identity. Are you holding on to inherited perspectives, or are you ready to grow with newfound wisdom? Are you willing to release outdated frameworks, liberating both yourself and your children from inherited constraints? Do you possess the courage to walk freely without crutches, unburdened by societal expectations?

As you progress in this exploratory journey, you will step into a realm that transcends conventional learning. Here, curiosity becomes your compass, guiding you through revelations and mystical truths that rekindle inner joy and vitality. Embracing these eternal principles will deepen your understanding, empowering you to approach life with renewed enthusiasm, an open heart, and an ever-evolving spirit of exploration. This journey fosters a mindset that celebrates growth, adaptability, and a youthful wisdom that remains receptive to life's wonders.

Therefore, it is essential to inculcate these timeless insights as an invitation to rise above past limitations, cultivating a soul enriched by the wisdom of ages and empowered to build a life anchored in harmony, health, and wonder. As you unlock these inner dimensions, you transform not only your existence but also become a beacon for generations to come, sparking a ripple of love, freedom, and joy that reverberates throughout time. In discovering the true essence of your celestial journey, you embrace your role in this incredible universe as a radiant vessel of light and boundless potential.

Let this moment mark the dawn of your legacy, a life that inspires, uplifts, and ignites the spark of enlightenment and superconsciousness, casting its glow across the world for eons yet to unfold.

Author's Note

The true understanding of how our minds operate and influence our lives must be embedded within the very foundations of holistic education and deeply rooted in family life. This transformative journey towards self-awareness and enlightenment must commence not only in classrooms but also at home. Even before a child is born, it is essential for parents to grasp the authentic purpose of parenthood, understand the critical importance of a child's first seven years, and embrace with open minds and hearts the deeper meanings of marriage, love, religion, spirituality, customs, traditions, and self-identity. True education involves the awakening of both the mind and soul, fostering an understanding that transcends mere intellectual learning to connect with the very essence of life.

This work presents the essential aspects of the inner science of body, mind, and soul—serving as both a valuable addition to school curricula and a practical guide for parents, teachers, and students on the path to holistic transformation. Such metamorphosis—encompassing mental, physical, and spiritual growth—should begin in early childhood and be supported throughout the schooling years by insightful, compassionate teachers and engaged, enlightened parents.

Building on this vision, this guide integrates teachings on inner science, psychology of the mind, and universal laws seamlessly into educational frameworks, ensuring young minds receive not only academic enrichment but also holistic development. By introducing foundational concepts such as self-awareness, emotional intelligence, and the recognition of boundless potential at an early age, children can grow into resilient, empathetic adults with a profound understanding of their eternal nature and an ability to navigate life with purpose and harmony.

Enlightened parenthood is central to this transformative journey. As first educators and role models, parents have a profound influence, reinforcing universal values within the home through love, empathy, and real-life examples. With an awareness of divine laws and an understanding of the mind's inner workings, parents create a nurturing space that fosters the child's development in all dimensions of life, preparing them for the journey of self-discovery and purpose.

The timeless law of sow and reap unfolds continuously in our daily lives. Teachers, parents, and grandparents who actively contribute to their children's journey towards mental, physical, and spiritual growth find that these same qualities blossom in their own lives. By sowing seeds of wisdom, compassion, and enlightenment, they cultivate a future abundant in harmony, prosperity, and fulfilment—not only for their children but also for themselves. This shared journey of growth and transformation will ultimately lead to a more enlightened, compassionate, and prosperous world for all.

To facilitate the practical implementation of this vision, I have spearheaded the development of the Path to Purpose (PTP) Global Mastership programme, a pioneering initiative that places the collaborative roles of pupil, teacher, and parent at the heart of its vision. This groundbreaking programme provides students with a holistic education that seamlessly integrates ancient wisdom with contemporary, transdisciplinary learning methods. Designed to help students uncover their limitless potential, cultivate unique talents, and develop essential lifelong skills, PTP emphasises personal growth, social responsibility, and global awareness. Spanning from nursery through high school, the programme delivers a well-rounded curriculum that integrates academic, creative, and physical disciplines, thoroughly preparing students for success across all aspects of life. By nurturing the triad of pupil, teacher, and parent, PTP fosters a supportive learning community where all three stakeholders collaborate to cultivate compassionate, globally conscious leaders and lifelong learners.

The triadic principle at the heart of PTP resonates deeply with sacred traditions across cultures. In Christian theology, it mirrors the Father, Son, and Holy Spirit; in Eastern spirituality, it aligns with the *trimurti*—Brahma (the creator), Vishnu (the preserver), and Shiva (the transformer); and in Islam, it reflects the relationship between Allah (the creator), the Prophet Muhammad (the teacher/messenger), and the Ummah (the community of learners and followers). These sacred triads beautifully align with the programme's central theme of pupil-teacher-parent, highlighting the universal interconnectedness and collaboration necessary for holistic development and meaningful personal transformation.

Educators, parents, and grandparents from all corners of the globe are warmly invited to Accra, Ghana, a place steeped in history and affectionately called the Gold Coast or Land of Gold. Here, they can witness firsthand the profound integration of the inner science of body and soul at Healthy-

Mind International School—an innovative institution I founded in 2021, dedicated to providing education for the future, rooted in the wisdom of the past. This sanctuary of learning harmoniously blends ancient wisdom with a futuristic educational framework, creating a transformative space where children can thrive.

From the very beginning, our students are encouraged to cultivate balance and mindfulness, equipped with the essential tools of contemplation, exploration, and introspection. These tools enrich every aspect of their personal and academic development, fostering an environment where their growth—both intellectually and emotionally—is nurtured. The curriculum extends beyond conventional education, incorporating arts, music, dance, gymnastics, swimming, tennis, football, organic agriculture, healthy eating habits, and yoga, starting as early as the age of three. These diverse experiences create a fertile ground for children to uncover and develop their unique, inborn talents and personalities, guiding them to unlock their fullest potential through dedication and discipline.

Much like the tennis legends Rafael Nadal, who began playing at the age of three and went on to win twenty-two Grand Slam titles and an Olympic gold medal, or Novak Djokovic, who started at age four and now holds twenty-four Grand Slam titles along with an Olympic gold, we, too, believe in the immense power of early nurturing. The same transformative journey is demonstrated by Carlos Alcaraz, who became the youngest player to win four Grand Slams by age twenty-one after starting at the age of four. These examples—though rooted in athletic achievement—serve as a reminder of the potential we all possess when we provide the right environment to cultivate and refine our innate abilities.

Today's true gold is our children, and every nation has the potential to transform into a Land of Gold by providing the necessary resources through an educational system that nurtures the innate potential of every child. This empowering environment will pave the way for our children to achieve extraordinary success, whether in athletics, the arts, sciences, or any field they choose to pursue. Imagine a world where each child's potential is realised, where their talents are fully cultivated, and where they are not only prepared for a career but for a fulfilling life.

This vision, though deeply practical in its call for enlightened parenthood and holistic schools, also demands that we confront the deeper shadows within our global educational systems. For while children are naturally born with infinite potential, much of today's schooling extinguishes rather than ignites their inner flame. This sobering truth is what I explore more fully in my companion work, *The Sins of Education*. That book holds up a mirror to the hidden distortions of modern education—its obsession with conformity, competition, and credentials—and reveals how these so-called 'sins' separate us from the true purpose of learning: self-realisation, service, and oneness.

Together, *The Mind Is a Labyrinth with Three Keys* and *The Sins of Education* form two sides of one sacred coin: the first decoding the inner mysteries of the mind, the second unveiling the outer structures that either liberate or imprison it. Read together, and practically embedded into school curricula, they chart a continuum of transformation—from the awakening of the individual soul to the reimagining of collective education—both converging on the conviction that education, when rooted in love, wisdom, and universal law, is not merely about preparing for a livelihood, but about preparing for life itself.

Join us on this groundbreaking educational journey and experience firsthand how we can shape the leaders of tomorrow. Together, we can ensure that every child has the opportunity to thrive and contribute to a world enriched with harmony, prosperity, love, and giving—values beautifully encapsulated in 'The Law of Reciprocation,' a poem that unfolded in my dream in 2001 and has become the cornerstone of our school song, sung by students and faculty each morning. The poem has been included at the end of this section to offer a reflective closing.

The law of reciprocation reminds us that when we give—whether it is love, honesty, or dedication—the returns are tenfold, multiplying in ways we may never anticipate. By embracing this principle, we cultivate a spirit of generosity and compassion, empowering every child to contribute their unique talents to a world in desperate need of healing and connection.

This is not just about fostering individual growth but about creating a global community united by shared values of kindness, respect, and unity. By embracing the law of reciprocation, we transcend the boundaries that have historically divided us, whether through religion, culture, or race. The universal truth of giving moves beyond all these differences, offering a common ground where the world's religions and philosophies can unite in harmony. In giving love and compassion freely, we align ourselves with the highest teachings of all major faiths, whether it is the Christian call to love thy neighbour, the Islamic concept of charity and community, the Hindu focus on compassion and selflessness, or the Sikh principle of oneness of all beings and equality for all. By embodying these ideals, we rise above the barriers that divide us and nurture the seeds of a more unified, compassionate, and enlightened world.

The Law of Reciprocation

When you give a little,
You get back a little bit more!
When you give a little bit more,
You get back a lot more!
When you give a lot more,
The returns sometimes are ten-fold!
So, giving is the key,
Love, honesty, and dedication are the chains.
And once you are filled with these emotions,
There will be no more setbacks in life,
Only promotions!
So, let's give love,
Let's give honesty and dedication,
To all those who are around us,
Let's cross the borders of religion,
And enter the world of God.
The law of reciprocation begins from Him,
The way He gives us without asking,
Let's give it back to Him.
And we can do that,
By giving a little, a little bit more, a lot more,

Love, honesty, dedication to each other.
Brother to brother, sister to sister, husband to wife,
And never forget our father and mother.
If we allow the law of reciprocation to work for us,
Then who can be against us!

Acknowledgements

The dawn of my life was illumined by the sacred love of my father and mother. Not only in my first seven years, but throughout my life, I witnessed not mere affection but a divine union. They never addressed each other by name; instead, they spoke the language of the soul—*pyareo*, meaning 'my love.' In this gentle rhythm of call and response—my father saying, 'Pyareo,' and my mother replying, 'Hanjee, pyareo,' meaning 'Yes, my love'—there resided a universe of tenderness, reverence, and devotion. From their love I came to understand what a true marriage means: two souls merging into one flame. That lesson shaped my own wedded life into a divine union of two lovebirds, as our friends so often called us, and now it flows onward as a golden current into the lives of my children—an eternal chain of love unbroken.

My foremost gratitude is to my parents, who revealed to me the essence of unconditional love and marriage without ever needing to utter a single word. Even in the final days of his earthly sojourn, my father imparted wisdom that remains engraved upon my heart. With quiet dignity, he asked my mother and her sister always to dress in bright, colourful garments—even in his absence—carrying the hidden message that love should not be clothed in mourning nor bound by the pallor of white or black, but should remain radiant and alive, shining beyond the veil of customs and tradition.

To the distinguished author Khushwant Singh, I extend my sincere appreciation. He became the bridge to two destinies: to my co-author, Ratanjit S. Sondhe, with whom *The Sins of Education* was born, and to Ashok Chopra, the visionary author and CEO of Hay House India, who discerned the light in this work. Without these connections, the path of this book, in its new incarnation, might have remained veiled.

A very special word of thanks belongs to Aditya Jarial of Hay House India—truly the wonder man—whose rare gift of editing refined this manuscript with such care, clarity, and brilliance that it now shines more brightly for every reader who turns its pages.

To my united family of oneness, at our home of love—the pillars of my being. To my beloved Mitthu, my heart's anchor and constant song; to my daughter Jasmin, who gives my works a home in the world through her publishing vision; and to my daughter Alipt, my voice and messenger, who now carries my flame of global educational reform through her works, travels, and leadership at Healthy-Mind International School, guiding the next generation into the light of purpose, service, and wholeness.

To all of you, my love and gratitude are boundless, etched not only upon these pages but upon the very breath of my existence. May this offering, born of love and shaped by countless hands, serve as a small flame in the great lamp of oneness, lighting the path for every seeker, every child, every parent, every teacher, and every soul who longs to learn, to grow, and to awaken.

About the Author

Gurdip Hari is a dynamic and accomplished individual who embodies the timeless truth that good health is the ultimate wealth and the gateway to experiencing heaven on earth. Since stepping back from business and public engagements, he has devoted his time to inspiring others to discover their life purpose, elevate health and well-being, expand consciousness, and promote world peace through advancements in health and education.

Through his books and teachings, he endeavours to awaken individuals' inner consciousness and empower them with potent creative tools to cultivate a body that defies age and a mind that transcends time. His overarching mission is to spark inner transformation from childhood, enabling future generations to emerge as revolutionary leaders in diverse fields and contribute to the creation of a peaceful, joyful, healthy, and prosperous world.

To bring his vision of educational transformation to life, he played a pivotal role in founding Healthy Mind International School in Ghana—a forward-thinking institution designed to merge ancient wisdom with modern pedagogy. The school's philosophy revolves around nurturing each child's true essence and innate talents, empowering them to become lifelong learners and excel as masters in their chosen fields.

Over the years, the transformative impact of his books has been evident in the countless individuals whose lives have been changed for the better. They have experienced significant improvements in their mental, physical, spiritual, and financial well-being. Kim Kascht, a resident of Arizona, USA, expressed her profound admiration for his works, stating, 'His books need to be in every household as his philosophies are inspirational and soothing, and I thank him for being generous with his spirit.'

Gurdip Hari's contributions—through his writings and visionary educational programs—continue to inspire a new generation of holistic leaders committed to creating a better, healthier, and more harmonious world.

'The gateways to wisdom and knowledge are always open.'

Louise Hay